COMMENTARY AND OTHER STUFF

AND EVEN MORE FRAGMENTS OF MEMORY

TOM MCCOLLOUGH

WITH
OCCASIONAL COMMENTS BY HIS
DAUGHTER
JANICE HUDSON

iUNIVERSE, INC.
BLOOMINGTON

Commentary and Other Stuff
and even more fragments of memory

iUniverse books may be ordered through booksellers or by contacting:

*iUniverse
1663 Liberty Drive
Bloomington, IN 47403
www.iuniverse.com
1-800-Authors (1-800-288-4677)*

*ISBN: 978-1-4620-1487-3 (sc)
ISBN: 978-1-4620-1486-6 (ebk)*

Printed in the United States of America

iUniverse rev. date: 5/5/2011

for my delightful daughters, Elizabeth and Janice

and a special thank you to
Bob Ballus
who read all the first drafts and made helpful
suggestions

Contents

PREFACE

Why on earth would I publish COMMENTARY AND OTHER STUFF, subtitled, "and even more fragments of memory" after writing VIN YETS. It certainly isn't to share my life with my children and grandchild. They already know most of the facts and lies, and only Alex, my grandson, might care someday. No, I publish these offerings because I can. My body is fading faster than my mind, and I wake up at night thinking of things I remember or would like to say.

Visions of immortality dance in my head. Imagine a grizzled scholar in 2050 wandering through the Amazon catalogue and discovering ISBN 14401842216. "Aha", he shouts, "I have found the holy grail of memoirs."…my modest history discovered years after the fact.

I write because I still can. I have a few relatives and friends who might be amused by these little pieces. Mark Twain declared that his autobiography should not be published for 100 years after his death, It has now been published, and reviewer Garrison Keillor suggests that Twain might better have thrown his notes and papers away. As unkempt, diverse and boring as those memoirs are, I enjoyed learning about what interested Twain day by day. Here is a secret. In VIN YETS I neglected to include a table of contents. From time to time I open that book at random and read a piece or two, and I experience a delightful twinge. Did I write that? Isn't that a hoot? Oh well, now you know.

Tom McCollough Saratoga, CA 2011

Aging Is Like Eating An Artichoke

The first time I ate an artichoke I was bewildered. My friend, Jim Jefferies, explained that you peeled off the leaves one by one, dipped each into the dipping sauce of melted butter and lemon juice, and then scraped the flesh off with your teeth until you got to the middle of the artichoke. There you would find a delicious mouthful of flesh called the heart. But beware. The heart has a choke attached to it. That part is inedible, and must be torn off and discarded. Only then could you enjoy the unadulterated heart.

Now as an old man, I have decided that eating an artichoke is a metaphor for aging. After seventy we begin to strip off a lifetime of things, activities and events that made life rich and interesting. Eventually, if you strip enough things away you are left with the succulent heart…yourself.

What do you mean "strip away"?

Old folks no longer covet things that we once thought were important, like clothes, for example. For years at work I wore classic grey flannel suit, button down collars and rep tie…to weddings, to church, to funerals, to parties. I wore garters to hold up my stockings, and for a while I wore suspenders. All gone. Now I wear an old pair of khakis, a polo or tee shirt and a sweater if it is chilly. No more ties, dress shirts, or knee high stockings.

Most household activities have disappeared. Someone takes out our trash. A certified nurse assistant makes our bed. So many things stripped away. Our meals are provided, so no more weekly shopping trips to buy food to feed the family. No cooking, no doing the dishes…just a handful of foods in the apartment to snack on. Shopping is reduced to a minimum. No house to care for. No lawn mowers or yearly weed killers to spray. No gas to buy for the tractor. No tractor. What serious shopping we do is done on the internet…mostly books and a few essentials like underwear, socks and slacks. If something doesn't fit, we toss it, or take it to the store where a nice tailor shortens the pants legs.

Regretfully, too many old friends are also stripped away. Every one of the original office staff I worked with is dead. Relatives are stripped away too. Nearly every usher I had when we got married is dead, including my brothers and college roommate, Greer Heindel. The flip side of the coin is that we make new friends, a network of names on my email list with whom I exchange regular messages, mostly jokes and occasionally a meaningful inquiry or observation.

Eating and foods require a lot of constraint. At lunch, soup and half a sandwich will do, with a ball of ice cream for dessert. At supper a baked potato with some form of meat and gravy is enough. I will have a sip or two of wine if offered, but a whole glass, and I am woozy and uncomfortable.

We no longer yearn for travel to exotic places. The airports and airplanes (or even cruise ships) no longer excite or beckon.

Travel is too damn much bother, and it takes too much energy, including going through two weeks of mail when you return from afar. Instead, we watch Rick Steves' travelogues. Enjoy him take the tram to the top of the mountain or eat in a tavern enjoying the local brew or dessert. Been there, done that.

Routine is our best new friend. Beauty is defined as following a regular routine through the day. Get up, watch some morning TV news, have a light breakfast, dress casually, go to lunch, do a crossword puzzle, have a nap. Read a while. Watch the evening news, eat dinner followed by Jon Stewart and Stephen Cobert, followed by some reading or computer games, and off to bed. Day after day, I seek simplicity. Of course we are still too busy…volunteer assignments, writing some more VIN YETS, doctor and dental appointments. But none that create much tension or worry. Just the essentials, back to the artichoke heart.

Tangible things have lost their allure. We have stripped away going to auctions to look for "things", to the theater to see the hottest new play, to the art galleries to buy something for the walls or piece of art glass. If people rave about a new play, buy it on Amazon and read it. No new trinkets have darkened our door in years. (Well not quite.

My new Kindle gives me pleasure and let's me pretend that I am still in the game.)

Now the $64 dollar question. Have I reached the real me yet, the essential heart of me? Has enough stuff been stripped away to qualify as the authentic Tom? Has the choke been chucked?

My ego is still strong, centered and content. No outrageous schemes lurk as "must do" or "must have." I feel like the frisky elderly lady on the first floor who has a sign on her door: "LET ME ALONE. I AM BUSY LIVING EVER AFTER." Or, maybe I am just another self-centered old fart.

SOME GAINS AND MOSTLY LOSSES

After eighty, life is mostly about losses. Loss of friends because of the grim reaper, or loss by memory. How many times have you said. "What was his name?" You can still see the face in your mind's eye, but cannot recall a name to go with the face. After friends, so too goes memory itself. Most of us experience forgetfulness, short of dementia… more an inconvenience than a handicap.

Do you remember the TV show starring Candice Bergen? A tableful of eighty-year-olds cannot remember the name of the series. Of course, "Murphy Brown."

Thank God for the internet. Type in "Candice Bergen" on Google and up comes the answer. I even remembered that Dan Quayle condemned the show because Murphy got pregnant without a husband. But her series name…a geriatric puzzlement.

Living in Assisted Living reminds one daily that many residents have lost their spouses, and as folks talk, you can sense their profound loss as they talk lovingly of their good and bad times together. One widow says, "We never agreed on anything, but it didn't make any difference."

Those who no longer drive say that giving up their car was the most serious loss of all. They now feel like shut-ins, and rely on the goodness of children, friends and the shuttle to take them out occasionally.

Physical mobility becomes an issue. Arthritis freezes knee joints. Muscles won't do what they used to do, and the threat of falling is a serious concern. Many have fallen, and the hope is that you won't break anything or hit your head. Canes, walkers and scooters become the norm, and hardware becomes a part of your body. Like pacemakers and knees. (And even eye lenses when they peeled off your cataracts.)

Hearing loss is common, and no one seems to like their hearing aids. A good hearing aid can cost $4000 an ear. WHAT! I can't hear what you are saying. It's OK, I wasn't interested in what you said anyway.

We even lose height. I'm four inches shorter. We have a pile of trousers on the dining room table to take to the tailor to cut off the unneeded length. I'm guessing that after the pants are altered, no one will notice. It would startle me if someone said, " I see that you got your pants shortened.!" Pant leg length just doesn't mean much to eighty year olds.

We lose the need for a tie. You used to wear ties to work, weddings and funerals, but I notice that people don't dress up for funerals like they used to. I keep my ties in the closet, but I can't imagine why.

Gains do occur. I can't remember losing sleep because of a recent worry. Worries are there, but not there. It's just that old folks can't be bothered with them any more. Just sit back. Things will either get better or worse, but what of it?

Old age brings a sense of quiet and of patient waiting. Routine is beauty. Want to upset me? Just change the order of things.

Don't Touch My Junk

Don't touch my junk. I mean it. I will have you arrested.

BACKSCRATCHERS

Three backscratchers are strategically placed in critical areas of operation. One is next to the computer. The second is by the couch where I am likely to sit. The third is by my side of the bed. Don't laugh. An itch is worse than pain. The most frustrating itches are located in the middle of my back where neither hand can reach.

KLEENEX

Lying next to the three backscratchers are boxes of Kleenex plus one in the bathroom. Each is associated with a different time of day. In the morning my nose is likely to drip. That's when the couch box is necessary. At bedtime, I blow my nose before putting on a sleep apnea mask. The computer warrants a box because I am there throughout the day and use the tissues as napkins to wipe off salt when I am eating cashews or peanuts.

PEN KNIVES

Ten years ago I started carrying a pocket knife. On our way to Florida we usually stopped at the largest knife store in America, the Smoky Mountain Knife Works. If I didn't buy a new pocket knife I paid $.25 to have a pen knife sharpened. Pen knives are always being lost. I keep one in my pants pocket. Three knives are located where I might need one to open an Amazon box or cut off a dangling thread…in the living room, in the bedroom on a table next to a reading chair, and by the computer.

HAND SANITIZER

Whatever happened to soap and water? Surgeons still scrub, but nurses pump up a little Purell every time they pass the dispenser. My hand sanitizers are located next to the couch, next to my iMac keyboard, and in the bathroom. Marian sometimes buys generic brands, and I struggle to figure out the tilting top to unleash a squirt.

PRETZELS, CASHEWS AND PEANUTS

Some of you may have favorite snacks when the hunger pang strikes at three or eleven PM. That is why I keep nuts and Hershey's kisses in the den. A box of Snyders Hard Beer pretzels is carefully located next to the reading chair near an open can of warm pop. (for hydration). For emergencies we keep a case of Snickers bars in the ice box, and a case of York Peppermint Patties next to the piano. We also keep apricots in stock for snacks.

STAPLER AND SCOTCH TAPE

After years of bickering, Marian and I each have our own stapler and scotch tape on our desks. Both items are used several times a month, and the equipment was always on the wrong desk, Now each has his own. BUT, where are the staples? I think Marian is in command of those, and I beg when necessary.

At my age, I am not concerned about a TSA agent fondling my junk. I don't plan to go anywhere requiring a plane flight. But I become a raging bull if anyone touches my "junk" at home. After every move to a new location it takes months to locate the things you use frequently. After living in #2137 for a year I have no idea where the toothpicks are, or a bottle opener. With luck neither will be needed in the foreseeable future.

Just don't touch my junk. Please!

A Woman's Response To "Don't Touch My Junk"
by Janice Hudson

As I read through Dad's Vin Yet, I realized that for women everywhere, I was required to even the score. Most men have this obsession with their "stuff", sometimes to a neurotic level. See, I'm married to one of those guys. This particularly applies to his Man Zone, the garage. For many years, if I even thought of using a tool, I was often met with "What do you need that for?" Followed by "that's the wrong tool to use", despite the fact we used exactly the same tool for a project the previous weekend.

I will give him, however, that sometimes I use a tool for a job that it is not intended for, but it seems to work just fine.

We have our separate 'junk' drawers in the kitchen. His drawer- inviolate. For many years it was verboten to even look in said drawer, while he felt he could rustle through mine at any time. It seems as if he might be hiding papers or secret weapons from the CIA. I cannot come up with any other explanation.

So we have an understanding. His tools- it's ok for use, as long as I put them back promptly and in the same place. So all is well. I do have to give him one point- MS hits us with cognitive changes, and often I get distracted and will leave his tools in the wrong place. This frustrates him, and I have to agree with him.

We have one small problem. For a while, Mark did some cooking, even being awarded a "Man Can Cook" binder with recipes. Then he considered my kitchen his kingdom, to which he had free rein. Trouble was afoot when he began to claw through my various kitchen implements declaring, "You don't need this, I'm going to throw it away". That was too much. "When was the last time you used this", he would ask, waving my potato masher in the air.

"About six months ago", I replied.

"Well, obviously you don't need this if you don't use it", he declared.

Now my beloved has a zillion tools squirreled away in the garage and tool shed. He prides himself on always having the right tool for any job. We'll be working on a household project, and suddenly he'll disappear. Grandly he'll stride in, waving the ERT (exactly right tool), saying, "I've had this for years. Figured I'd need it one day".

The fact that my kitchen tools serve the same purpose seems to be lost on him. When I point out that even if I haven't used something for a while, I still expect to find it when I need it.

Final Point, Gentlemen. We'll stay out of your stuff, only and only, if you stay out if ours.

WITH JUST A HINT OF
BLACK CURRENT

Drinking wine is a phase we all go through. And we must master the rules, and there are many rules. How to swirl and examine the legs, how to sniff, how to sip, how to examine the cork, how to match the wine to the food, how to pick among the myriad of choices (Californian, Australian, French, Chilean, South African). How much to pay. You also have to learn wine-speak. Zinfandels are "zins", cabernets are "cabs", chardonnays are "chards".

Percent of alcohol is no small matter. Too much (17%) and the wine loses its mellowness. Too little (10%) and you might as well drink warm water. Mastering the vocabulary of the nose takes years of practice. "This is wine in which the grape is forward, but with aroma of strawberry, heather and with just a hint of black current." (As if we knew what a hint of black current smelled like.) And never forget the tannins. "Needs more time the age. Should be laid down for another five years."

You also need to understand terroir, the ground in which the vine is grown.

Once aboard the Radisson Diamond we had a port call in Bordeaux. The featured day trip was a excursion to sauterne country… a small geographic region about twenty miles by twenty miles where the famous French grapes are grown. The most famous of the vineyards, Chateau Y'quem was closed that day. But the bus driver drove into the winery anyway so that we could genuflect at the place creating one of the most famous (and expensive) wines in the world. We drove then to the next vineyard down the road, and had a tasting. The sauterne was similar to the more famous wine and nearly as expensive. We bought three half bottles. We were startled when the short, pink-cheeked, beret-covered winemaker whipped out a portable phone, and swiped our credit card.

That night we were invited to a hyped $600 dollar dinner at a "famous" Bordeaux winery. We were asked to wear formalwear with sneakers…to be explained later. Arriving at dusk we were served champagne in the gravel courtyard (explaining the sneakers.) Following the hors d'ouevres, we were ushered into a dining room nearby. We were seated elbow to elbow in a cramped space that was 100 degrees. We waited and waited. Someone came in to open the windows to let in the humidity. And we waited. The men took off their tux jackets, and we waited.

Eventually a first course of a catered dinner arrived. It was of no account.

The dinner was a complete bust. The four courses were at least an hour apart, and completely forgettable. The wines were mediocre. Marian and I had been given a freebie because we were such good customers of the cruise line. The people who had paid $600 were apoplectic, and close to riot. The next day the cruise line apologized and removed all charges for the dinner.

And so…what about Two Buck Chuck? There are no legs, It is a blending of leftover wines from many wineries, and it pleases many faithful wine drinkers. It does contain enough alcohol that you can truthfully admit to your doctor that you have two glasses of wine a day.

But only God knows what terroir it came from or how to describe its nose.

MOONLIGHT IN JAKARTA

Many moons ago I had a Dutch friend who worked for Abbott, at first in the Ross Division, then in the International Division. Eventually he was stationed in Jakarta to manage the pharmaceutical plant and sales force there. Hans Voorn was a delight. Tall, stately, with thinning blond hair, he had the slightest tinge of Dutch in his English speech.

Sometime in the early eighties I was sent to Jakarta to meet him to discuss market principles we were using in the United States. Those principles were based on the marketing theories of Ernst Dichter, the father of modern motivational research. Dichter's primary message was that assuming that a product was useful or necessary, the company that made the user's life more interesting and efficient would achieve favor. For example, he recommended that cake mixes require the addition of an egg by the housewife to "involve" her in the baking process. He defined the automobile as a sex symbol. Our company provided many services for doctors in the cause of being a "helpful ally."

Arriving at the airport, I took a cab to the Hilton Hotel in downtown Jakarta. This was the first time that I had been in a country below the equator, and I was curious to know whether the moon would be upside down from its appearance in the northern hemisphere. The doorman at the hotel was garbed in one of those calf length wrap around sarongs that I had seen in the movies, It was all very exotic.

After dinner when it was dark I walked out into the garden to view the moon. I was disappointed that the moon appeared exactly as it was in Ohio. Jakarta seemed less exotic from that moment.

The next morning Hans picked me up and drove me to the plant in the suburbs that he dubbed "pharmaceutical row." Pfizer, Wyeth, Lily and several others had their manufacturing plants within several miles of one another. We toured our facility briefly, including the small mosque where Muslims prayed several times during the work day. After the tour we spent the rest of the day discussing marketing practices in Indonesia.

Hans was an old friend, and he asked me to stay for the weekend so that he could take me sightseeing. He picked me up the next morning and we headed for the hills. He wanted me to see his childhood home about fifty miles away. His father had been the mayor of the town. The roads were well built and safely paved. He explained that Suharto's wife owned the Mercedes Benz franchise in Indonesia, and that all the busses were Mercedes Benz. Suharto saw to it that the roads were properly built to protect his wife's investment.

From time to time we passed or were passed by an open truck packed with smiling ladies…tea pickers Hans explained. I drank tea but had never seen a tea plantation. We passed several on the way. The tea bushes were a little less than shoulder height, and hordes of ladies in the tea orchard were busy picking the new leaves off the top of the bushes.

We arrived at Hans' hometown. It had been the seat of Dutch Colonial governance when Hans was a boy. The town had a smattering of lovely but disheveled old one story stuccoed homes among a mish mash of old and new. "That is where I lived before the Japanese invaded. That was the jail where we were incarcerated during the war." His pleasant tone never changed, and he made that pronouncement as a simple matter of fact. Apparently he and his family were not too badly treated. He said nothing more about those times. I wanted to hear his story but thought it best not to open old wounds.

To this day I marvel that the moon is right side up in Indonesia.

DOES THE QUEEN LIKE PARSNIPS?

Conventional wisdom claims that British food is lousy. That may have been true during and before the war, but it is no longer true. Every little town has a sophisticated vegetarian restaurant. Delicious continental food is everywhere, and green grocers specialize in exotic and local produce. A worthy green grocer will feature perhaps eight varieties of apples, although you are not apt to find our big round gelatinous apples that Americans favor.

The Brits still cling to some curious food and drink… shandy, for example. Once made with lemonade and beer in equal proportions, it is now bastardized by mixing beer and Seven Up. Shandy is the biker's drink for restoring fluids during and after a long hard bike ride.

Lamb is a favored meat in England, but the British mint sauce is an acquired taste. It is simply made by combining water, malt vinegar, sugar and mashed or chopped mint leaves. It may be served cold or brought briefly to the boil and simmered until the flavors are blended.

Do you know about bubbles and squeak? It is not about Beverly Sills and Mickey Mouse, but a traditional favorite made with left over boiled cabbage and mashed potatoes mixed together, sometimes made into patties and pan fried, but just as often stirred together and warmed.

Mashed potatoes find their way into many dishes. The most well known is shepherd's pie, a meat pot pie topped with mashed potatoes rather than a pastry crust. In recent years, the meat has often been ground, making it a hamburger pie, less regal to be sure.

The British breakfast table most likely has a contraption for holding toast, called a toast rack. It sounds a bit pagan, but the toast is usually served cold accompanied with slabs of butter and jam. When the bread, white or wheat, is firm and substantial, the toasted bread is as hearty as a meat course. If you put meat between two slices of buttered toast, the combination is called a "meat butty."

Hot oatmeal is a frequent breakfast cereal, but most families have Wheetabix in their larders. Wheetabix comes in fist-sized patties. When milk is poured over them they turn into a sweetened mush like soggy Wheaties.

At tea time a luxurious treat is revealed…clotted cream and scones. The phrase "clotted cream" sounds ominous, but is to die for. Cream is placed in a pot in a water bath, and warmed for hours and hours. The cream slowly evaporates and becomes thickened until it becomes a spread. When eaten with a freshly baked scone it is rich and delicious, but not oily like warm butter. Think thick whipped cream, but much better.

In rural England lunches reflect the rural setting with the famous ploughman's lunch…a hard roll with a big hunk of butter, an apple and a thick slice of cheese, usually cheddar. In fancy restaurants, they might also add a cornichon or gherkin pickle. A cookie is often included for dessert.

If you eat lunch in a pub you will encounter the Scotch egg…a hard boiled egg wrapped in a savory meat blend, rolled in crumbs and deep fried. With a "pint" you can enjoy your lunch standing up. Or, you might have a bottle of cider with your Scotch egg. American cider is either unpasteurized apple juice or pasteurized and filtered apple juice. In England the juice is allowed to ferment. The result is alcoholic, tart and malty.

The following describes mortal sin in a dessert bowl. It is called Sticky Toffee Pudding. It is a type of luscious moist cake made with dates, flour, cream, eggs and sugar over which a caramel sauce is spooned, and set under a broiler until the caramel bubbles. It is a diabetic nightmare but who cares. You must try Sticky Pudding before you die. The British are said to consume more sugar than any population on earth. Most of it is in one serving of the pudding.

I am told by a reliable friend that I have missed two staples of traditional British food…Toad in the Hole and Spotted Dick. Toad in the Hole is sausage or other meat baked in a batter. Spotted Dick sounds like a venereal disease, but is simply rolled up dough with dried fruits, baked and served in a bowl topped with custard.

One vegetable that never made a successful transition across the pond is the basic parsnip…part white carrot, part turnip, part potato. Sometimes they are mashed with cream and butter. Sometimes bite-sized pieces are boiled and buttered. Sweet when mashed or roasted, slightly more flavorful when served whole. It is a veggie with no excuse for existing, at least in my mind. I cannot remember a single time when my children asked for parsnips.

I suppose the queen likes them. She's very British, you know.

How To Leash A Non-Compliant Teenager

Parents want their children to learn to be independent. But when they behave that way we have hysterics, at least Marian and I did when Janice, our youngest daughter started making her own decisions.

I suppose every family has rules about what time the children are due home after teenage parties on weekends. Darkness spells trouble when youngsters are out at night, coming home on a bike, or with the family car. Mothers and dads do not sleep until they hear the car door slam in the driveway or the front door open, no matter the age of the child.

Janice just celebrated her 50th birthday, and she went kayaking. When she hadn't returned after three hours, I went to her husband and said, "I am worried about Janice." "She'll be all right," he reassured me, and of course she was, but I still couldn't suppress that vision of the kayak turning over, and her not being able to wiggle out of the boat. My concern will never fade. I am her Dad.

During high school, we would set specific target times for returning home…ten, eleven, rarely twelve. "If you are not going to make it, call us so we know that you are OK." And she often did.

A downtown Palo Alto movie house had a midnight showing for teenagers. I would never let Janice go unless I agreed to drive her friends and her to the theater and sit among the clouds of pot. Janice insisted that I sit somewhere else in the theater so that she would not be embarrassed.

On one particular night she was going to a friend's house for a party. We set the time for arrival home. At the appointed hour she called and opined that the party was just "getting going" and wanted to stay longer. Knowing that I would not sleep until she got home, we set a new target time, several hours hence.

At the appointed time, no Janice. Two hours later, no Janice. My anger became real worry as we fidgeted, and thought about the coming confrontation when she would arrive. Threats? Grounding? Withdrawal of telephone rights? Then the idea struck.

Let us call all her friend's parents and ask whether they had seen Janice. Of course the parents were asleep, and answered no, they had not seen Janice. I trust I caused some of them to check whether their own child was in bed.

Janice came home safe and sound, and our "confrontation" was rather mild. We did not mention the telephone calls we had made.

After school on Monday, Janice came noisily into the house screaming, "WHAT DID YOU DO?"

"We roused all your friends' parents out of bed to ask if they knew where you were."

"DON'T EVER DO THAT AGAIN!"

"Don't ever come home late again."

And she never did.

REFLECTIONS ON THE UNDERWEAR BOMBER

The main stream media has displayed countless pictures of the explosives sewn into the Nigerian bomber's underwear. How charming. If the bomb had gone off, and the man blown to smithereens, would he still be equipped to handle the covey of virgins he was supposed to acquire for being a martyr? This recent incident has triggered a lot of underwear memories.

For example. my mother, all of five feet one inch, and a bit over 100 pounds, wore girdles. As they wore out, she would pull out metal stays and give them to me. I pretended that they were drumsticks. A kitchen pot made a marvelous drum, and I spent hours practicing my paradiddles.

Dad, on the other hand wore one-piece cotton BVDs. They were a sort of tank top attached to a boxer bottom going almost to his knees. I think they had a drop seat, but I never really paid attention to that.

Why is underwear called "unmentionables"? Is it because underwear is associated with sex, and it is sex that is unmentionable? Or, that we do not walk around in our underwear. (Although we troop around on the beach with practically nothing on.)

And why on earth did Bill Clinton answer the question whether he wore briefs or boxers. He should have said that is was none of the questioner's damn business, and then dropped the subject. But in the era of "transparency" he answered, briefs. When the Monica Lewinsky scandal broke. It was her thong that excited the president to reveal his briefs.

By tradition Navy seals wear no underwear. I have a friend who never wore underwear. That seems strange, doesn't it? One wonders whether these folks change their pants everyday. I assume that most people change their underwear daily.

That was not always the case. In medieval times the citizen was sewn into his underwear in the fall, and unsewn in the Spring when it was warm enough to take a bath. This was the reason for perfume use, we are told. When I was a little boy in elementary school, our underwear was good for a week, and then we had the inevitable weekend bath, and fresh clothes for the following week.

And why is black underwear considered sexy. Mother always said that she would love to own some black underwear, but could not afford any. For my 50th wedding anniversary, some close friends gave me a set of black underwear. And I admit that I felt like a dude wearing the stuff. When my white underwear wore out I ordered only black replacements.

But, don't ask me whether I wear briefs or boxers. It's none of your damned business.

THE MOST BEAUTIFUL
THIGHS ON EARTH

It's Sunday afternoon. I am on a weekend pass in San Francisco. I have several hours to kill before thumbing a ride back to Camp Cooke. I am walking down Market Street when I spot a handsome 1920s movie theater. The marquis announces an afternoon performance by Josephine Baker, the Paris-based American chanteuse. Not knowing what to expect I take my seat to await the performance.

Josephine Baker is as famous as Edith Piaf, but for different reasons. Yes, she could sing those lively French love songs, but she is best known as a dancer, dancing nude, wearing only a skirt of fake bananas. She was a world famous star of the Follies Bergere and in Paree jazz clubs. During the second war she was a member of the French underground, sending coded messages in her music to the allies. She was honored with the Croix de Guerre, and made a member of the Chevaliers of the

Legion of Honor. In later years she started an orphanage, and adopted dozens of children.

The theater was nearly full with a typical Sunday afternoon audience: mostly families, and many children. After a movie, the stage show began. Baker sang, danced and chatted with the audience and received a wonderful ovation. The backup band was excellent, playing its jazz with energy and strong syncopation.

As the show was coming to a close, Baker invited all the children in the audience to join her on the stage. Twenty or thirty kids came up, and Josephine started dancing, and asked the children to do the same. One by one she sent the kids back to their seats until she was down to one who was mimicking her movements with uncanny accuracy. Then a second show began. She sang and danced encore after encore, with the little girl shadowing every move. It was magic, and the audience roared with approval. This was the definition of pure entertainment. We cheered and clapped, until finally it ended. And those thighs. I had never seen such wonderful thighs.

During the Twenties many Parisian artists drew posters for Baker's shows, nearly all in the Art Deco mode. Her long legs were always exaggerated. Small pointed toes, swelling to a smooth gastrocnemius, and then flowing to a nude, voluptuous thigh.

In the early Seventies, Baker returned to the States to raise money for her orphanage. When they announced the dates for her San Francisco appearances, I immediately bought tickets for the show. I wanted Marian to see the great lady, and I wanted to see those memorable thighs again.

Sadly, the show was an enormous disappointment. The voice was gone, and Baker could not remember the lyrics. Little 3 x 5 cards were posted all over the set with her words and cues. She included several of her orphan charges in the show, and their talent was minimal, compared to the little girl on that Sunday afternoon. Baker danced, but not with great vigor. Her costumes exaggerated her long legs.

But at sixty years of age or more, she still had those stunning thighs.

Things Disappear,
As If By Magic

Things disappear from common usage, but are usually available on the internet. Here are a few examples.

We never had servants at home, but mother frequently set the dining room table with a silver-plated crumb brush and tray. She never brushed crumbs, but it sat there as a symbol of elegance and of a previous era when a maid would brush the table before dessert and coffee. I don't recall seeing an ad for a crumb set in 70 years.

Type in "crumb brush" on Google and you will find pages of them for sale, and many ancient authentic ones at auction on eBay. I suppose there is an army of crumb brush collectors out there panting to own a real one from the Thirties.

At expensive, overpriced restaurants one can expect to be crumb brushed before the final course. If you see a crumb brush being used, you can assume that you have paid too much for dinner.

Also disappeared…as a child we always had a small blue and white pack of Campfire marshmallows in the pantry. We ate them as snacks, and of course at bonfires, stuck on the end of sticks. It is a great art to roast a marshmallow to the perfect degree of brownness before setting it on fire. The melting fluff would be so hot that you had to wait a moment before popped it in your mouth. If it did burn, you ate it anyway, even with that wonderful burnt sugar flavor.

Someone will undoubtedly remember S'mores. But we never made them in my family. The toasted, virgin marshmallow was sufficient at our bonfires.

eBay offers very early packaging of Campfire marshmallows, when they came in tins. Marian and I can only remember the little blue and white paper boxes containing eight marshmallows. I cannot find a photo of one of those, but I am looking. Our primary use for marshmallows was for hot cocoa or eaten raw as a snack after school. And like potato chips, you could never eat just one.

A serious loss to my diet is the Cheese Tidbit cracker, sold for a dime in a box the size of animal crackers boxes. A Cheese Tidbit was in the shape of a small hot dog, and the size of a licorice Good and Plenty. A handful were delicious additions to tomato soup, but they are no longer sold. A year ago I had an interesting exchange with the Nabisco company who produced them. I opined that I loved them and missed them. Was there any chance that they would be put back on the market? The answer was clear…NO, "once a product is removed from the market place it is almost never brought back." How sad!

Do you remember sugar cubes? British films would feature a tea drinking scene with the question, "one or two lumps?" Restaurants in America often had them on the table, but rarely anymore. (They did take a little work to stir them in to a cold glass of iced tea.) I don't miss sugar lumps the way I miss cheese tidbits.

Many other items from our past have disappeared. Do you recall those bulky recorders with the wire spools. These proceeded "tape" recorders with real plastic tape. They went the way of all flesh to the wireless, electronic voice recorders. But if you really covet one, you will find one on eBay.

Finally, one way we could raise a little pocket money as a child would be to turn in returnable glass bottles for a nickel or a dime. Mother always had a brown paper bag at the back door into which all empty soda bottles were placed. Every Saturday the bag would be taken to the grocery, usually as a down payment on the next week's returnable bottles. I confess that on many occasions I would go up and down the back alley looking in people's trash for the glass booty.

When people say, "the more things change, the more they stay the same," they lie. Everything changes except in politics when you are trying to garner enough votes to pass a bill…a vote can still be bought. Elsewhere, everything changes.

Let It Snow, Let It Snow, Let It Snow

Blizzards are not uncommon in central Ohio. In 1978 we had a REAL blizzard: four feet of snow, wind gusts at 50 miles an hour, and drifts on the road up to ten feet, impenetrable.

We lived in a 100 year old farm house that had no insulation. Gas heating was possible with gas from an oil well. The electricity came in over the wooded hill, and frequently went out in storms. In short, the house was not a safe place in a blizzard. Marian and I worked in Columbus, Ohio about 40 miles to the west.

The night before the storm the weather had been warm, above freezing. Through the night we could feel the temperature dropping, the wind coming up, and some snow turning from big juicy clumps to dry flakes being driven sideways by the wind. Before dawn Marian and I agreed that we better leave the house promptly before the lane and country roads became impassable. We put extra cat food in the basement, and left.

At that time we were driving an International Harvester 4-wheeled-drive Scout. By the time we got to our little village, the visibility dropped to zero, We were in a whiteout. I asked Marian to roll down her window and guide me along the berm, but she couldn't see the berm by now. Becoming alarmed, I decided that we would take County Line Road west instead of of Route 204 that had many twists and turns. We turned right at the Frizzell farm to drive north to County Line Road. It was still dark, and I had zero visibility.

In half a mile I drove off the road into a ditch with the Scout leaning perilously to the right. The car stalled. Trying again and again, I could not restart the car. We were stuck. Soon we would have no heat, no food and inadequate clothing. We agreed that we should abandon the car, and walk to the Frizzell's, half a mile away. We could barely see the house in the distance and we started walking. My cap blew off, and I wrapped a scarf around my head. We were dressed for work. I was wearing oxfords.

We pushed ahead. In a few minutes Marian called to me and said, "I can't make it." I have never hit her, even in anger, but thought something serious was needed. I put on my deepest, most severe voice and screamed, "Get going." She moved on. We got to the back door of the house. Henry and Jetty Frizzell still had electricity, and they were sitting at the kitchen table.

The Frizzell's had recently had a robbery. A stranger knocked at the back door, and while they were talking another robber entered the front door, and helped himself. Jetty opened the door and stared at us. "Our car went off the road, and won't start. We live on the Torbert property, and the weather is too bad to try to go back." She unlocked the screen door and let us in. Henry looked appalled.

The Frizzells were probably in their late sixties, and lived modestly in a red brick farmhouse dating from the mid 19th century. The kitchen was large. The center hall had a living room to the left, and a parlor to the right. Behind the kitchen was a summer kitchen with a second stove for canning and baking. Henry had a reputation as being a gruff non-talker. Jetty was the sweet prayer-lady at the Christian radio station a few miles to the north. She would take calls on the air and pray with you or for you, whatever was needed.

Within a few moments she became affable, went to a drawer and returned with a blue knitted cap with a large pom-pom on top to replace my cap that had blown off. "I knit these for people who need them." At daybreak the topic of food came up and she disappeared. Dour Henry sat in his parlor chair without saying a word. In fifteen minutes she called us to the kitchen and had the table spread with a complete hot meal, canned roast beef, mashed potatoes, green beans with rolls and butter. After a passionate grace we ate heartily. When we finished the entrée, she arrived from the summer kitchen with a two-tiered coconut cake with thick butter icing. About then the electricity failed. The storm had worsened, and we knew we couldn't leave, but we were safe in the arms of a fundamentalist evangelical couple.

The house began to cool. Henry knew the pipes and radiators would soon freeze. For the first time Henry spoke directly to me. "I need to shut the furnace down and drain the pipes. Come to the basement with me." He found flashlights and we inched down the rickety wood cellar steps. The furnace was a huge old coal furnace that had been converted to gas. Henry asked me to hold a valve open while he did something on the other side of the chamber. I hoped he wasn't finding a axe to chop my head off. He was not then or ever friendly.

By mid day we settled into a routine. Every hour or two, we made a prayer circle, held hands , and prayed that the wind and snow would stop, and that we would be safe. The Frizzells had a grown son named Joe who had a bulldozing business . He arrived on a bright yellow bulldozer, hooked up two gas links from a nearby well. He lit a small gas heater in the parlor, and another line to the summer kitchen stove. Meanwhile, Henry erected blankets over all the interior doors to stop the drafts. Evidently, we were not to have cocktails before meals, and the elderly Frizzels thought that coffee was the devil's soft drink. But Joe had brought some coffee so that Marian and I could have a cup at breakfast.

That first day passed slowly, with the wind still howling, and the snow steadily making the deep drifts even higher. We looked out the frosted windows, but saw no traffic on the road. The phone still worked and each hour we called the Glenford firehouse to get the latest status report, and the best gossip about who was sick, or who refused to leave their homes. The national guard was trying to clear the roads to the west, and the state highway patrol was trying to get to us from the east and south. We were truly marooned.

The first night, Jetty announced that we would sleep upstairs in her bed. Henry planned to sit up all night in the parlor. I supposed that she would sleep on a couch, because no heat reached the second floor. Marian and I slept fitfully under four or five blankets and a comforter. As soon as the dawn light broke we got up, dressed, and went to the kitchen. Jetty was already up and (bless her heart) had made coffee for us.

By the end of the second day the storm had passed through, and we began to wonder how we could leave, and where we could go. Snowplows were now passing the house, piling up drifts ten feet tall by the side of the road. I fretted how we could get the Scout out of the ditch, and whether it would run.

The next morning, neighbor Bob Palmer, knocked at the door and said he had just pulled our car out of the ditch. Did we want to find out if it would start? It did, and we returned to Jetty and Henry to thank them and say goodbye. I tried to pay them for the lodging and food, but they refused to take any money. Henry was finally talking a little, but one sensed that he was very glad to get rid of us.

Jetty said we should have one more prayer. We had prayed hourly that the snow would stop, and that the winds would subside. Her last words to us were, "See, our prayers were answered." I didn't have the heart to say a word about storm patterns.

James Joyce, And My Friend, The Spy

The Army has a place to billet soldiers who are waiting for orders for new assignments. They are called "replacement depots" (Repple Depots in Army slang), and they are sometimes called "casual units." While I was awaiting for orders to be cut for infantry OCS at Ft. Benning, I was assigned to a Replacement Depot at Ft. Ord, California.

When assigned to these units, the Army tries to take care of mundane administrative affairs, dentist appointments, updating shots and all other matters for which there is no convenient time on a regular duty assignment.

Because the unit is bound to disappear promptly, close friendships and interpersonal relationships are not common. My time at Fort Ord was unusual because I forged a relationship with another person waiting for his orders…John Znerold.

While in the Army I spent a lot of time reading books. John noticed me reading, and one day he came over to my bunk and told me that he was a teacher with a doctorate in English literature. Had I ever read any James Joyce? I replied that I had not, and wouldn't know where to start. The teacher voice bloomed, and he said I should start by reading "The Dubliners." That should be followed by "The Portrait of the Artist as a Young Man." Then and only then would I be prepared to tackle "Ulysses." Finally, and if I was still interested, he would suggest delving into "Finnegan's Wake" last. His conversation concluded that he would also suggest reading something by Ford Madox Ford, a contemporary of Joyce when both of them lived in Paris.

Over the next few weeks, John revealed a few bits of information about himself. He had come to California to study Russian at the famous Language School in Monterey. His previous assignment was at Langley, Maryland. That's all. LANGLEY…hmm…CIA. Russian language school plus CIA equals American spy in Russia, at least in my mind. He did not reveal where his next assignment would be.

Nor did I take his advice on James Joyce. The first book I read was "Portrait of the Artist." I found the writing a bit spacey and ethereal. Then I plunged into "Ulysses" and I was in for a big shock. Nothing could have prepared me for that adventure. It was unlike anything I had read before…hundreds of puns, literary and historical allusions and thousands of far out, made-up words.

Only years later did I read "The Dubliners." They are imaginative, lucid and interesting short stories that are easily grasped with some of the most beautiful sentences ever written in the English language.

In my mind's eye, John was the only spy I would ever meet. Before we parted he gave me his mother's address. After I had read some Joyce, I wrote to him to tell him what I had felt about it. I never received an answer. He obviously was serving time in the gulag, and didn't receive my mail.

As for Ford Madox Ford, poet and novelist, I never have taken the time to read anything by him, even his most famous novel, "The Good Soldier." But I did bump into him in several places. He is discussed negatively by Hemingway in the book about his young years in Paris, "A Moveable Feast." The famous bookstore in Paris, Shakespeare and Company, run by Sylvia Beach, has it's own fascinating book, "Sylvia Beach and the Lost Generation," with many references to Ford.

It's a small, circular world. It was Sylvia Beach who published "Ulysses" when no other book publisher would. I am grateful to John Znerold for explaining how to read Joyce, if John ever existed.

HOW TO EMBARASS
YOUR MOTHER-IN-LAW

Our wedding day was September 10, 1955. A doctor who shared Marian's father's Manhattan office offered to host a dinner in his west side two story apartment the night before. The entire wedding party was there. Marian's family lived in a wonderful big old stone house in Yonkers. After the ceremony in a nearby church, the reception would be held in the yard. I came in from Columbus, Ohio a few days early, and spent my time planting flowering chrysanthemums to gussy up the lawn.

The night before the wedding we all gathered down town Manhattan for an elegant supper. When the meal was over it was decided that my brother, Jim, would take over as my caretaker until the wedding. The Brown's had arranged for the wedding party to stay at the Rockledge Manor, a residential hotel in downtown Yonkers.

The dinner party broke up, and Jim and I drove to Yonkers. I never wrote down the name of the hotel, but it seemed easy enough to remember. It was a dark and stormy night, and visibility was limited. We turned onto the correct street, and then I saw a sign, Wayland Manor. "This is it I hollered," and Jim parked the car. By now it was one o'clock in the morning.

The night clerk was housed in a small enclosure with one light burning over his head. I said," We are Tom and Jim McCollough, part of the Brown wedding party. We have reservations. He stared at us, looked at the register, and said he could not find us. I repeated the names of some of the others...Dr Jack Filer, Greer Heindel (my college roommate), Edythe McCollough (my mother). He just stared.

"OK", Jim said, "just give us a room and we will straighten it out in the morning." He wanted cash.

Jim and I crawled in bed and tried to sleep. That's when we started to hear the click, click of high heels in the hallways. Click click, all night long. Jim and I had registered at the best little whore house in Yonkers.

In the morning we showered and shaved and left for the Brown's. I was to dress there, but according to tradition was not to see Marian.

When we arrived, Marian's mother came to the door, and looking grey said, "Where have you been. We've been worried to death about you." "We were at the the Wayland Manor, and they didn't have us listed."

"The Wayland Manor?" She was ashen. "Never, never tell anyone were you were last night." I thought she was going to faint.

This matronly, women's club type who once hosted Eleanor Roosevelt, now was on the precipice of utter social embarrassment.

We didn't tell.

You are the first to know.

As Time Goes By

We are attached to the wide world with computers, but it wasn't always so. Before television we had boxes in our living rooms called radios. The radio was on morning noon and night. In the morning we got the weather, the important national news, and local traffic reports.

At noon, depending on the era, you listened to the noonday soaps…Stage Door, Helen Trent, Our Gal Sunday that asked the question, "Can this girl from a little mining town in the West find happiness as the wife of the wealthy and titled Englishman, Lord Henry Brinthrope?" After supper it was Alexander Woolcott ("The Town Crier"), Amos and Andy and best of all, "I Love a Mystery" featuring a squeaky door. If my wife misbehaved as a child, she was not permitted to listen to the "Lone Ranger." Now that's punishment. Sunday night brought Jack Benny, Fred Allen and then Charlie McCarthy.

The box in our living room was a big wooden console Philco with a celluloid dial. The knob to move the dial was broken, and you changed stations with your finger rotating the cylinder. We were expert. The radio was on almost all the time.

Just before dinner each night the networks broadcast serials aimed at children, with sponsors selling products for youngsters, such as Wheaties and Ovaltine, the milk additive. If you sent in six tinfoils under the Ovaltine lid, you received a decoder ring. After each Little Orphan Annie at 5:30, the announcer would recite eight or ten numbers to be decoded, spelling a clue about tomorrow's show. I would not miss an episode…and I hated Ovaltine.

There's more. We listened to serial mysteries such as the Green Hornet and The Shadow Knows. On Tuesday night we enjoyed comedies… Fibber Magee and Molly followed by The Great Gildersleeve.

These days, the only radio we listen to is when we are driving in our cars. Our car came with free XM radio for a few months. That meant that we had access to 100 clear channels, and we eventually subscribed, but only listen to two stations…the classical pops channel, and the humor channel, the one with the clean comedians. If you care to, there are two smutty humor channels where you can listen to unending foul mouth barrack's talk all day and night.

People now carry cell phones, Blackberries, wi-fi lap tops, iPods and lord knows what else. I sometimes think that if messages were visible, the air would be filled with hordes of gnats flying every which way. Railroad operators "text" away on the job, neglecting to slow the train, crashing into oncoming trains. And, all that equipment is expensive. We are in a recession, but myriads of kids call their friends endlessly all day, and the parents pay the bill.

For decades I earned my living with a pen and a pad of yellow paper. My boss called us together one day and said, "I've ordered computers for every one. From now on we will have a secretarial pool, and you will do most of your own typing. Bad news...I never learned to type, and I had never used a computer. The first computers were Wangs, then IBMs with constantly changing software. I felt like Sisyphus pushing a rock up a steep hill. Later we bought an Apple PC for home use, and went through the agony of choosing a server, learning how to surf the net, receive and send e-mail, and play Solitaire.

If computer traffic were visible in the air, the sun would be obliterated with those pesky gnats. They say that cell phones are safe to hold next to your brain. Could those skillions of internet messages somehow penetrate our scalp. Is that why there is so much angst in the world? Or, is it that we are just overly wired?

Right now I am trying to decide whether there is any benefit to join Facebook....free, of course. This could be the work of the devil.

THE 2010 OIL SPILL: WHO'S RESPONSIBLE?

When the offshore oil well blew up in the Gulf of Mexico, was Obama responsible? When Katrina flooded New Orleans, was Bush responsible? When the volcano blew up in Iceland, was Icelandic President Grimsson responsible? When we have an earthquake in Saratoga, will our executive, Kate Ledford be responsible for the tremor?

These are events over which our political leaders have no control. But we search for culprits, and we find them everywhere. Assessing blame has its merit, particularly legally. Who will pay the bill? Were any crimes committed? Regarding the oil spill, the government agency, MMS (Minerals Management Service), apparently let the oil companies fill out their inspection forms in pencil, and the bureaucrats filled them in in ink (if they had a moment while watching porn at their desks, taking drugs or accepting tickets to the Peach Bowl.) Pundits blame

Dick Cheney for the spill because he had been the CEO of Halliburton.

Rumors abound as we search to assess blame. The oil spill is not a natural phenomenon. It was man made. Some want to make it Obama's oil spill. The media spinners think that if Obama goes to Louisiana and makes a speech while grubbing in the oil gook, he will fix the problem like Moses parting the water. Can't happen. A fine speech will not solve the problem.

I once had responsibility for crisis management where I worked. When something goes wrong, things get complicated in a hurry. You must think of customers, distribution systems, media, and most importantly, finding the origin and solution to the problem. In one case it became necessary to prove a negative, a semantic and technical nightmare.

When things go haywire in large organizations, managing the problem internally is one of the toughest problems: who needs to know what, who has a stake in the issue, who will make decisions, particularly if resources are needed quickly? (Most middle level executives don't have the fiscal authority to spend a million dollars.) Meetings become a nightmare. Assume there are 14 stakeholders in the meeting…scientists, lawyers, quality control people, marketing staff, public relations experts, executives with authority and responsibility, etc.

Each person wants to talk to explain the crisis from their point of view. Hours pass. In the case of the 2010 oil spill, hundreds of meetings went on across the globe, all with different points of view. Tensions mount. Meanwhile the spill gets worse, and more meetings are called.

Let's look in on the first crisis meeting in the White House. Rahm Emanuel calls the meeting in the Situation Room. The participants arrive, about twenty persons…the president, admirals, crisis managers, oil regulators, lawyers, politicos, scientists, engineers, etc. The crisis manager briefs everyone first and then Obama invites comments from the others. Each gives his or her prospective. An hour passes. David Axelrod says, "We must appear to be on top of the crisis, but we don't want the problem to be our responsibility, especially because the leak may get a lot worse." After more talk, a frustrated Obama says, "Just plug the damn well." Meeting over, with the agreement to meet each day at four until the worst is over.

Now imagine you are the CEO of British Petroleum in London. His meeting with 20 participants begins with the engineers telling everyone what happened and the current status. Then Anthony Hayward, CEO of BP invites the others to explain how they see the problem. The lawyers say that perhaps they can deflect the blame to Halliburton or Transocean, minimizing BP's role. The scientist and engineers explain their approaches to capping the well in Louisiana. The finance officer says that the costs will be significant. If BP is blamed, maybe three billion dollars or more. The public relations people say that a decision must be made whether to have BP speak from England, or set up the press releases and spokesmen in Louisiana. Hayward says that BP should set up an on-site command headquarters immediately in New Orleans. After more discussion, the engineers are authorized to build a giant steel dome to put over the well to collect and siphon off the spill.

Suggestions to solve the problem are made by the thousands. Shrimp boat fishermen want to go out to sea to scoop up oil, but they can't. There is a law that people who handle hazardous substances have to be "trained" and credentialed. Bureaucracy gone amuck.

The media are demanding.

"What's going on?"

"When will the well be capped?"

"Who is responsible?"

It is said at the White House briefing, Obama is reported to have opined, "Plug the damn well." He had it right. Everything else is irrelevant. "Plug the damn well" is the only position that makes sense.

At the same White House briefing, Joe Biden sat quietly next to the President. As the meeting broke up he hollered, "Plug the freaking hole."

May, 2010

PAINTINGS

Our senior high school trip in 1946 was to Washington, DC. One morning was spent in the new National Gallery, then just five years old. One room was devoted to the Dutch artist Vermeer. So began a lifetime of trying to see all 34 of his paintings. In fact, that trip began a lifetime of collecting, studying and appreciating art. It set into motion visits to many important museums, haunting sales galleries in New York and buying local or regional artists wherever we lived.

Marian and I both worked, but we were salaried and never had much disposable cash to buy art. Buying big name artists was out of the question, although it was exciting to visit Madison Avenue galleries and look at Picassos, Gauguins and Matisses for sale. Our first purchase coincided with the birth of our first daughter, Elizabeth. We hired Anna Schreiber as housekeeper when Marian and Tish returned from the hospital. One evening when I drove her home, Anna said that she wanted to show me something in her apartment…a closet full of paintings by Leslie Cope, a competent regional artist who lived in Roseville, Ohio. His realistic paintings were of rural countrysides, many with horses. Within a year we bought "Winter Morn" for $40, and we were off and running.

As important, we met Leslie and became friends, a friendship that lasted 40 years. As we acquired more art, we befriended the artists...Bill Kortlander, Keith Boyle, Jack Piper, Barbara Chavous, Jonathan Kaufman and others. Most artists haven't much money and welcome a patron who will buy and pay monthly. Before long we had a house full of art.

People ask, "What is good art?" I have a fool proof answer. Art is good if you want to steal it. I saw a Van Gogh drawing of an almond orchard and literally imagined I could take it off the museum wall and run with it under my coat. The only way to acquire an experienced eye is to look, look, look at art wherever you are... London, New York, Los Gatos, Amsterdam, San Francisco, Manila. et al.

"Good" paintings have several characteristics: they usually contain something that is surprising or unexpected. Also, they must have staying power. Even after ten years a "good" painting will still please you, and you will enjoy looking at it. You might even find something new that you had not noticed before.

Some ways of learning about art are dead ends. We subscribed to Artforum, Art in America and Art News, but most of the articles in magazines are puff pieces about current shows, and are rarely critical of the work. LOOK at art. Reading doesn't help much.

Talk with people who love and collect art. Babs Sirak had enormous wealth to buy multimillion dollar paintings: Degas, Monet, Nolde, Klee and dozens of others of museum quality. More importantly, she told us about a remote museum in Holland that is off the main path but contains one of the largest collections of Van Goghs (272 paintings and drawings) not in the Van Gogh Museum in Amsterdam. The museum is the Kroller Muller Museum in rural Holland. You can see his early masterpiece, "The Potato Eaters" and "Terrace of a Café at Night" in a wooded, quiet setting near Arnheim.

Bill Kortlander taught painting at Ohio University. He recommended going to the Tate Gallery in London to see the fabulous Turner collection; these paintings were painted about 1800. Some of Turner's most famous paintings look as if they were painted yesterday, impressionistic as the French painted 150 years later.

Sometimes artists become friends who will let you see their work in progress. Jonathan Kaufman came to the States every four years usually during the presidential elections. He toured the United States in a rented car, with his folding stool and a watercolor set. As he traveled he would sit in small towns, paint local scenes that people would buy, thus financing his trip. He stayed with us before and after his road trips, painting or drawing every day as we watched a painting emerge. We have visited Jonathan in London and Shrewsbury, England. We stay in touch weekly by e-mail.

My quest to see all the Vermeers took a downward turn when the National Gallery in Washington started removing their trove, relabeling them as "in the school of", or in the "manner of." The Rijkesmuseum in Amsterdam has several, and the Frick in New York has three Vermeer beauties including, "Mistress and Maid." Unfortunately, today's Vermeer might be tomorrow's fake. Some experts have been fooled.

Art is a mystery. How much is art worth? Answer: whatever someone is willing to pay. Art fads come and go. Yesterday's hot painter may disappear in a flash, while an unknown is suddenly discovered, and collectors line up with salivating dealers. Is art merely decorative? Or is some of it of deep cultural significance? Think of the cave paintings in Lascaux, France, said to be 17.000 years old; or the paintings in Pompeii, both erotic and fanciful.

Why does a human decide he or she is going to be a professional "artist?" How many artists actually make a living? Is art for the ages? Does it have a purpose?

When all is said a done, five thousand years from now archeologists will dig through our flotsam and jetsom and find some chards and perhaps a bronze or two from which the academics will describe our lives back in 2010. Museums as we know them will probably not exist. 3-D web sites will present art projected life size on wall screens. You will never have to worry again whether you have hung a painting at the right height, with the right light, or whether it is hung straight.

Art is fleeting. Our collection has been through two downsizings, donations to museums, and gifts to our children. We miss some pieces that have gone…a recumbent nude by Bellows, for example. But we are fleeting too, and I am told that you can't take it with you.

Too bad.

THE VERDI REQUIEM, TWICE
BRAHMS REQUIEM, ONCE

The first time I heard the Brahms Requiem I was stationed in Bad Nauheim, 25 miles north of Frankfurt, Germany. A large Lutheran church was located in the center of this quaint spa town. Signs around town announced the concert as the first time the Requiem would be performed in Germany after World War II. The orchestra was the Frankfurt Philharmonic.

We rarely consider that 6.5 million Germans died in the war, including the German Jews murdered in the Holocaust…a total nearly one tenth of the entire German population. The country's young men were decimated. In 1953, a pall hung over the population.

On the night of the concert I took my seat in the balcony of the church transept and the audience entered, nearly all dressed in black. The scene was somber, and the air of sadness palpable. The Church was jammed, with no room allotted to separate the orchestra and chorus from the listeners. Not an inch of floor space was seen. After a glorious concert, a smattering of applause, and people left without speaking, too moved to talk.

Using words alone, how can I tell you about the Verdi Requiem?

Verdi wrote Aida, La Traviata, Otello, Rigoletto, Falstaff and about twenty five more operas. He IS Italian opera, written in the mid-1800s.

When Rossini died in 1868, Verdi had an idea: get twelve of his fellow composers write a Requiem Mass, each to write a section of the Catholic mass for the dead. He sketched out a section of the Libera Me. The project never came off but it was not forgotten.

When the Italian humanist, writer, and philosopher Alessandro Manzoni died, Verdi decided to write a Requiem Mass by himself. Following the text of the Roman Catholic mass for the dead, he completed the work which was performed in 1874 in Milan, Verdi conducting.

Verdi was a declared atheist; his wife a staunch Catholic. Verdi's mass that followed the Roman Catholic text was a great success from its first hearing. It is scored for a huge orchestra, double chorus and four soloists. It begins with a whispered choral entry, "rest in peace." It soars to a gigantic, thunderous rolling climax in the Dies Irae (Day of Wrath) and ends with a quiet plea for forgiveness. It is not an opera, but is operatic. One of the arias for tenor voice, Ingemisco, soars to a high B flat at full voice. Chilling.

Many years later in Columbus, Ohio our church choir scheduled the Verdi Requiem as part of our annual concert performances. Our choir had 85 voices. The Director, Dick Johnston, had studied conducting with

Pierre Monteux. Looking back, it is amazing that we were able to do it. Dick hired a brass ensemble, bass and kettle drums, with organ for the string passages. The four soloists were professionals living in Columbus.

The Sanctus is comprised of a double choir singing against one another at top speed with a crashing finale. It took weeks to sort that section out, but was finally mastered. We gave two performances with a packed sanctuary of 2000 each. Our organ had 32 foot bombards, and the vibration when they were sounded pierced your body.

Years later we were in London after the civil war in Nigeria. When Biafra seceded from Nigeria, the Nigerians launched a bloody police action to reclaim the territory from 1967 to 1970. Two million people died from the fighting and starvation. Public sympathy was with the Biafrins, and money was raised around the world to provide needed aid.

The Verdi Requiem was performed in St. Paul's Cathedral as a fund raiser. We took our two daughters and sat in the balcony. The church was packed. Full orchestra, huge chorus and four excellent soloists

St. Paul's was designed by Sir Christopher Wren and construction begun in 1675. It is massive, and famous for its weddings (Diana) and funerals (Churchill). But, it has a quirk. It is so large that the echo is said to be 11 seconds, not a place to enjoy the Verdi Requiem with its complicated choruses , frequent sotto voce passages and thunderous fortissimo highlights. In short the Requiem was "mushy", but beautiful, nonetheless.

By now I could "sing along", but the reverberation of the echo was so confusing that I sat in silence during the performance.

Today, if you audition for the leading tenor role in a Verdi opera, the music director will ask you to sing two brief passages…the final notes of the "Ingemisco" from the Requiem, and the final notes of "Celeste Aida" from Aida. It is assumed that if you can do both successfully you are qualified to get the part.

BOOKS

When I was growing up our neighborhood drug store had a lending library. Mother read best sellers, and she would go to drugstore and put her name on the waiting list for a "hot" book. Dad worked at the Philadelphia Evening Ledger. The paper received book review copies. Dad brought them home if the paper did not plan to review them. I remember "Native Son" by Richard Wright, among others.

The first book I ever received as my own was a Christmas gift from Aunt Helen or Aunt Tootie. It was a story about a ten year old in a circus environment. I was befuddled. I never had a book of my own that wasn't a schoolbook. I tried to read the book again and again. I'd get to page twenty and balk. What was I supposed to expect? Why read a book? Who were these people? Why were there so many pages? I treasured the book, and kept it in my bedroom, but never finished it.

In high school we were given book reading assignments such as "Silas Marner" among others. Some students devoured them and seemed so smart when we discussed them in class. The people never seemed real to me. They were fictitious and distant. Reading was work, even intrusive.

So when did I discover books and invest myself in them?

When I was drafted, I found the reading list that I was supposed to have read for Dr. Harbison during his cultural survey course at the University of Pennsylvania. I stopped at a bookstore and bought a Modern Library copy of "War and Peace", the first book on the list. For several months I carried the heavy book under my army tunic, and read a few pages during each hours' ten minute break. For the first time in my life a book transported me. I was there at the Battle of Waterloo. I practiced saying out loud the names of the Russian characters. The pronunciations were probably incorrect, but I knew who they were. Then I read "Madame Bovary", "Crime and Punishment" and twenty other masterpieces. Now I was hooked because great writing captured me.

From that time in 1951 I have read a book or so a month. I prefer non-fiction to books of fiction, for reasons I do not entirely understand.

Some books are read to entertain, to kill time or to edify. An Agatha Christie mystery lasts exactly as long as the flight between New York and London. Generally I do not enjoy what might be called a "book club" book. There are exceptions. After starting "The Help" I couldn't put it down, and often read when I should have been sleeping.

Occasionally a book has such an impact on me that I vow to read it every five years until I die, and I have. One said book is only 83 pages long, entitled, "Zen In the Art of Archery" by German philosopher, Eugen Herrigel.

After retirement, my reading has increased to a book a week. I read classics and best sellers such as "The Girl With the Dragon Tattoo". I read books I should have read years ago, such as "The Hound of the Baskerville." Last year I found a book entitled, "1000 Books You Should Read Before You Die." Goodness gracious, it's not possible. Last week I read, "Cleopatra" by Pulitzer-winning historian Stacy Schiff and volume one of Mark Twain's posthumous autobiography published 100 years after he died. Twain's writing is flecked with genius and captivates.

Reacting to a good book is very personal. I hope YOU have had that wonderful feeling that comes when you become completely absorbed in great literature.

It ain't sex, but it is very, very good.

The Good Book

Think the 1960s...flower children, the Vietnam war, transcendental meditation, "Let the Sunshine In", the Beatles going to India to learn from Maharishi Mahesh Yogi. Zen Buddhism is all the rage. A new way of living. Mastery and personal peace in a nutshell.

Easily said, but not easy to attain. Why? Because Zen masters do not proselytize. They know that the Western mind is wired for action, movement upward, control and accomplishment. Zen is an enigma, and centered in far off Japan, and Japan is also on the upward path. It doesn't compute.

Few books about Zen are written in English, the most famous by Alan Watts entitled, "The Way of Zen." Watts, in turn, was influenced by scholar D.T. Suzuki who taught at Columbia before returning to Japan where he was considered a national treasure.

In the spirit of the 60s, I started reading about Zen, but never found a book that satisfied my curiosity, until I found a small paperback of 83 pages entitled, "Zen in the Art of Archery" that finally gave me a glimpse of what the discipline is about. In the parlance of the day, "It blew me away", and I decided I would read the book every five years until I died. And I have.

The author, Eugen Herrigel was a German philosophy professor who was asked to teach in Japan for five years before returning to Germany. He and his wife decided that they should take the opportunity to study Zen. Their inquiries were rebuffed because the Zen masters told Herrigel that because of his education and life style he would never understand the Zen philosophy...but he persisted through new Japanese friends who suggested that the only way into Zen would be through taking up a Zen art form, namely swordsmanship, flower arranging (ikebana), or archery. She chose flower arranging, and he chose archery.

The archery master was very doubtful of success, but agreed to start. What followed was a five-year struggle to master a single shot that was in true Zen tradition.

Ask a baseball pitcher how he pitched a perfect game, or what he "did" to achieve the feat. He usually says he has no idea...it just happened. Before the scandal, Tiger Wood's golf game was beyond normal...week after week of extraordinary performance. Great musicians like Horowitz went beyond technique, and became one with the music.

Herrigel began his lessons. Months of learning how to breathe while drawing the bowstring, months of learning to pull the bowstring back while his shoulder muscles were completely relaxed, notching the arrow, and then the most difficult of all: letting the arrow go "when it was ready" and NOT a moment before. Herrigel complained that he never knew when the arrow was ready to be released. The archery master explained that he should think of snow falling from a bamboo leaf. At the proper moment the snow would fall to the ground effortlessly. That was the proper moment to let the arrow loose.

During the summer, Herrigel practiced at home in Germany and finally decided he knew when to let the arrow loose. He was eager to show his teacher what he could do. At the first practice in the new school year, the professor let the arrow fly as he had practiced. Zen master, "Show me that again." After the second shot, the teacher turned his back and sat down. Herrigel had made a fatal blunder. He was still trying to control the shot. The master refused to go on, and Herrigel realized how seriously he had insulted the master. Only with the intervention of Japanese friends did they return to instruction.

Months later when Herrigel was still practicing the "release" the teacher said, "Shot again, please." He did, and the teacher remarked that the lesson for the day was over, that the two shots were true. Herrigel did not know what he had done.

Now we approach Zen and life. We practice and practice (we live day after day for years). When we are hungry, we eat. When we are tired we rest. Life controls us, we do not control life. We go with the flow and go about our business naturally in good times and bad, and life brings some of each.

Professional writers tell you they know when "it is going well" as Hemingway remarked. The words flow effortlessly, and the author is amused and delighted at the output. Let a writer think too much, and writer's block sets in, and writing is struggle. Art should be artless.

Our story ends well. The next phase of learning concerned aiming at a target...no, not aiming, but hitting the target after years of practice, even in the dark. Eventually the Zen master said after five years, "You are ready for your test, but do not think about it. Just do what you do." The test was performed effortlessly, and Herrigel was presented with a certificate. "But how will I continue when I go back to Germany?" "You will never lose what you have attained. Send me a photograph occasionally so that I can see how you are doing. And as memento, here is my bow. Use it, but never share it, and when you are done with it, burn it."

All this and more in 83 pages. Some explanation is made of the art of ikebana, and of sword play. The same patterns of learning pertain. Learn the technical issues, practice, practice and practice until the art becomes effortless, until the arrow hits the shooter.

Memory, Not Memories

You know you are getting old when the only actress you recognize by sight is Meryl Streep. As you pass your Seventies you begin to notice that memory starts to fade away. Faces that once were your clue to names begin to look unfamiliar in the photo albums. You sometimes can't remember where you put the keys, or where the car is parked at the mall. (Answer: in your left pocket, and in handicapped parking,) Oh well, if you are patient, it will all come back…maybe.

The other night at dinner we were talking about giving to charity. I started to tell the story of a wealthy man who gave his money away to charity. I launched into the story of how his widow gave me (The Red Cross) $250,000 to start a "bank" in Columbus. What kind of bank? The words eluded me. "You know, an umbilical cord blood bank, No that's not quite right. Cord blood that can regenerate tissue. You know."

Gratefully, the woman across from me said, "Stem cells."

"Yes, we opened the first stem cell bank in Columbus, Ohio."

How humiliating. One of my favorite anecdotes, and I couldn't get it straight. Am I becoming demented, or just getting old? I prefer to think I am getting old, but one can never be sure. My mother had an advanced case of Alzheimer. She once said to me, "I am going crazy." When does dementia become "crazy?"

Our table partners laugh at least once a day at our failing memories. Is this Wednesday? Where were you at lunch today? What did you order for dinner? How do you feel today?

The answer is usually, "I dunno know."

When the little old lady was stopped by the police for speeding, the cop asked, Where are you going in such a hurry?" She replies, "I have to get there fast before I forget where I was going." So when does forgetfulness become dementia. I suppose it is when forgetfulness affects behavior. Whoa now. You are getting too close for comfort.

Table #31, A Study In Memories

Residents enter Assisted Living facilities because their bodies are in disrepair or they have some dementia and are not safe to live alone. Other reasons explain moving in. Sometimes a spouse becomes ill, a couple moves in, one dies, and the remaining spouse chooses to stay in the assisted living setting. In other cases, the grown children become concerned and insist that elderly Mother or Dad need to be looked after.

After a bad health year in 2009, Marian and I realized that we needed more protection from further complications. Marian requires compression stockings for the rest of her life, and neither she nor I can put them on. Now every morning a CNA (Certified Nurse Assistant) comes in, pulls on the stockings and makes our bed. Our laundry is done. They take out our trash every day, and our meals are provided. Almost every one living here is in their eighties, and some touching 90.

After moving in, time is needed to sort out the new life, and how to cope with the population of residents. Some minds are sharp as a twenty year old, while others are literally mute during meals, unable to carry on a normal conversation.

We stumbled onto Table 31 by chance. Table 31 seats six, and usually seats the same six people…George, Jim, Lois*, Marie, Marian and Tom. For reasons not entirely clear, the chemistry among the six is comfortable, casual and supportive. Occasionally one of the six is away at a doctor's appointment or on an outing with relatives or friends. Someone else joins the seating, and the atmosphere is immediately changed, often creating long periods of silence.

Otherwise, we chatter away like teenagers. We laugh, sometimes too loudly, and we receive stares from other tables. We talk about ourselves and our long lives. Marie worked for the telephone company. George was raised in Berkeley in a house up 48 steps from the street. Lois and her husband went to Hawaii for vacation every year. Jim was raised in Climax, Michigan, and is our naughty boy. He is a classic Type A personality, and is always dreaming up some wild-eyed scheme. Marian has the reputation of telling stories that get longer and longer and longer until eyes start to roll. I've garnered a reputation as Mr. Know-It-All. The truth is that I don't know it all, but Google does. When our memories get stumped I employ a search engine to search forgotten material, and bring printouts to our next meal to fill in missing or unknown facts. For example. last week we discussed Amelia Earhart. Was she married, was she flying solo when her plane went down? Answers: Yes and No.

All of us have some forgetfulness, primarily short term memory. Have we ordered yet? Did I order that? What day is this? (Thankfully that answer is printed on each day's menu) Last week I could not remember the words, "cornish game hen" when we were discussing a chicken entrée.

What binds us most are memories of the popular culture from the 40s to the 80s. None of us could remember the name of the third Andrews Sisters. Patty, La Verne… and who? Google revealed "Maxene."

Marie likes to stay up late and watch David Letterman, but we remember and discuss Jack Paar, Steve Allen, Johnny Carson and Dick Cavett and their guests.

Jim played the trumpet and saxophone in his military academy swing band. Consequently we gossip about big bands, their vocalists and histories. Do you remember Louis Prima and Keeley Smith? (Is it true or false that Prima abused Smith?)

All of us enjoyed Dean Martin, his guests and his roasts. A few months ago Table 31 went to Jim's apartment after dinner to watch a tape of Foster Brooks routines, and later Lily Tomlin. We have a DVD of Jonathan Winters waiting for Jim to make his DVD player work.

The usual six members of Table #31 are close enough that we can tease one another, laugh at our individual foibles and shades of forgetfulness. We call Marie "Precious" because her husband Jim did so when he wanted to "shut her up." Tom made up a sign for the wait staff: "MARIE DOESN'T WANT BEETS ON HER HOUSE SALAD." George has a classic Type B personality, quiet, passive and relaxed. But George doesn't miss a trick, and his subtle bon mots light up the place.

The point is…even at eighty (and beyond) you can create a new life of spontaneity and pleasure. Thaaaat's all, folks!

* Lois died suddenly of a massive stroke on January 2, 2011. Her unexpected death made all of us feel empty and vulnerable. Her chair is still often unoccupied.

WHO IS YOUR FAVORITE "WHO"?

"If you were stranded on a desert island, who would you pick as companions?" Or, " If you died and had to spend the rest of eternity with three companions, who would you choose?" (Sounds like Sartre's "No Exit.") A journalism student is taught that the who, what, where and when should be included in the first paragraph of a news story.

Surely an old man could answer the question, "Who is your favorite author?"

"Who is your favorite musician?"

"Who is your favorite painter?"

"Who is your favorite friend?" (Excluding spouses and children.)

"What is your favorite food?"

At eighty, one would presume that your opinions would be fixed, and that you could answer. But no, life is a kaleidoscope, and with each turn of the lens an opinion changes. What was number one yesterday might be last today.

At ten, Gershwin was my choice of favorite composer. At twenty, I thought Stravinsky and Rachmaninoff were tops. I vowed never to fall back on the three Bs, but I did, and then discovered Mozart, and the contest was over. Then another discovery. I bought all the symphonies of Sibelius and listened intently, and then all the symphonies of Mahler. Wagner was unknowable, but came into focus with tickets for Bayreuth. For a while my favorites were Gabriel Faure, Ravel and Debussy. Oh hell, the point is made. We go through phases in life and all things change constantly. Is that a sin?

Take painters, for example. In the pantheon of modern artists Picasso is supposed to be tops. He has been in and out favor at least five times. If you examine only one period, you might draw the wrong conclusions. Some of his weirdly distorted wormlike paintings of people do not fairly represent his oeuvre. No, you must look at his lifetime of work. Go to his museum in Paris or Barcelona and you will be stunned with the scope, energy and brilliance of the work. Picasso drew as competently as Leonardo did. His sculpture and ceramics are inventive and fun. The scope is breathtaking.

My favorite classical artist is Vermeer. When I first saw the Vermeers in the National Gallery in Washington there was a room full of them. Long since, most of them have been declared "in the school of" until they have been whittled down to a precious few. At the National Gallery…"The Women in the Red Hat." At the Frick in New York…"Girl With Maid." In the Rijksmuseum in

Amsterdam, a few more, including several that are not characteristic.

Looking at the "Girl with Maid" at a distance of five feet, the art is photographic. At a foot away…nothing but impressionistic smudges. Go to the Tate in London to see the late J.M.W. Turners. On first viewing you would swear they were painted in the mid-1920s by an impressionist. No, he was born in 1775 and died in 1851.

The winner for sculpture is Rodin. His most famous work is the "Thinker", but if you want a real treat, go to see the Rodin's at the Palace of the Legion of Honor in San Francisco, You'll see some wonderful erotic art that is tasteful as a Puritan wedding. Go to the House of Commons in London. On the lawn outside, across the street from Westminster Abbey you will discover a life size casting of "The Burghers of Calais." The array of six or seven larger than life figures is the epitome of strength of character.

This Vin Yet could go on for a dozen pages, but I won't press my luck. What is my favorite food?…hot dogs, baked beans, pumpernickel (with real butter) and cole slaw. Some of my tastes are plebian.

WHO WAS WALT SHERIDAN?

Ted Kennedy died last week, and we had four days of wall-to-wall television coverage of his life and times. I listened carefully, but I never heard the name of Walt Sheridan, not even once.

Senators with Kennedy's tenure and committee assignments had large staffs located all over the Hill. It was said that Kennedy's staff numbered 200 people in the late Seventies. Rarely were people given a private appointment with Ted, but it was easy to get an appointment with a member of his staff. I spent a lot of time with Walt Sheridan, a trusted confidant of the Kennedy family.

His association with the Kennedy clan began with Bobby, then Attorney General. Walt was the chief federal investigator of the Teamsters Union and Jimmy Hoffa. Walt was a lawyer, and had close ties with the CIA, the FBI and NBC. (He resigned from the FBI over Hoover's attitudes about communism.) In short, Walt was one of those nameless persons of enormous influence in Washington. He studied conditions in mines, the exploitation of farm workers, tampering of drug data at the FDA. He made recommendations for legislation to the Kennedys. When Bobby and John were murdered, he became a member of Teddy's staff.

Three American companies became ensnared in the Nestle infant formula controversy…Wyeth, Bristol Myers, and Abbott Laboratories, all of whom sold infant formula overseas. Nestle was the major target of the campaign generated by the National Council of Churches, and a group of anticapitalist activists who formed an association called INFACT. Their claim: the companies were killing babies in the third world for a profit…a very powerful message.

Fueled by the activists, the controversy had reached national awareness via television shows headlined by Geraldo Rivera and Bill Moyers. The New York Times and Time magazine picked up the story. Each of the American companies had hostile shareholder resolutions every year for five or six years.

I was in Palo Alto, working for the school district. The President of Ross Labs, a division of Abbott called and said, "We want you to come back to the company. The job we have in mind entails international travel, interaction with activist groups, and policy formation. "We will build a staff for you if you need one." Before long I learned that I was in charge of handling the infant formula controversy for the corporation.

The activists had interested Ted Kennedy's staff in the issue, and he was contemplating holding congressional hearings. Our Washington office recommended that we cooperate with the Senator, and I was sent to interview a member of his staff…Walt Sheridan.

Walt was a quiet man, very patient and non confrontational. I had no idea that he was known as one of the toughest, and some say, the meanest investigator in Washington. It was said of him that he dealt in unauthorized wire taps and even bribes to get information. By now I had taken several trips to Africa, the Phillipines and Central America to see the situation first hand and was well informed. I had amassed nearly 6000 documents about infant feeding practices in Third World countries. In short, I was a fount of data.

Walt Sheridan and I became good friends. For a year or so I saw him every other month for questions and answers. He informed me that Kennedy had decided to hold congressional hearings with the three American companies and Nestle testifying. I wrote the briefing books for the hearing. Our president, Dave Cox would testify on behalf of Abbott with me at his side.

I soon learned that congressional hearings are carefully scripted, rehearsed and ritualized theater. The questions are written, the answers also written and rehearsed. The order of the witnesses is negotiated, times specified, etc. The senators who are known to be friendly are given questions to ask.

A week or so before the hearings the three American companies met in a Washington hotel to sort out each others' testimony. These were sensitive meetings because of anti-trust issues. We were accompanied by a horde of lawyers to make sure we didn't cross that line of collusion. We were startled to find that at lunch that day a group of Nestle executives appeared saying that they had rented a room near ours just in case we needed them. I suspected that the representative from Wyeth had tipped them off to our meeting.

The day before the hearing I got a call from Walt. He said that Nestle would take the brunt of the Senators' wrath, and that we should relax and keep a low profile.

The hearing room was already packed when we got there. Sure enough, the senator asked us to submit our written testimony for the record rather than read it. After a few perfunctory questions. the senator became apopleptic, red-faced and derogatory about Nestle's behavior overseas.

At the end of the hearing Walt came to me and said that in three weeks, the Senator would like to see us privately. The date was arranged, and the three American companies with our legal entourages gathered in a senate meeting room.

Senator Kennedy entered the room with his entouage and said, "You guys are getting a bum wrap, and I know something about bum wraps. I have decided to turn the whole thing over to the World Health Organization in Geneva. I ask that you cooperate with the WHO. Walt will keep me informed."

Little did we know that the activity at the WHO would prolong the issue another five years with mountains of continued bad press. We had thought that the WHO was a scientific organization where data would prevail. It is not. It is a highly politicized organization filled with intrigue and back room deals. At the first meeting I ever attended of the General Assembly they spent a whole day with Arab states condemning Israel, trying to get their WHO health clinics shut down.

Walt Sheridan died in January 1995. His obituary in the New York Times was long and detailed. He was best known for the conviction of Jimmy Hoffa, He was best known to me as my fleeting link to Ted Kennedy.

POSTSCRIPT

When Secretary of State Dean Acheson was asked what he thought of Anthony Eden when Eden died, Acheson said, "Do not speak ill of the dead." When I wrote the circumstances of my brief, passing encounter with Ted Kennedy, I decided not to comment on the bad things that Kennedy had done.

But in avoiding the controversy, the VIN YET lacked the main message of my experience, i.e., that the Kennedy clan often resorted to "dirty tricks" to get their business done. When we were interacting with Walt Sheridan, Ted Kennedy was a red-nosed alcoholic philanderer, thirty or forty pounds overweight, with a failed marriage and lofty personal ambitions. He was ruthless in his quest to succeed, and was surrounded by a staff of yes men who did his bidding.

The real story of our interaction is that Kennedy double crossed us, and while cozying up to us in private, was causing us mountains of bad publicity, hundreds of thousands of dollars in out-of-pocket expenses, and hours and hours of executive and staff time coping with his efforts.

In his later years Kennedy reformed, and became even more "holier than thou."

Dying, he wrote to the Pope to "pray for him." A papal spokesman later said, " Kennedy is not known to us."

Things are not always what they seem.

EXACTLY HOW MUCH ARE ONE WIFE AND TWO DAUGHTERS WORTH?

If you are a conspiracy theorist, you would be very suspicious of the Union of International Organizations, founded in 1907, and headquartered in Brussels, Belgium. Its purpose, to enable communication among all international organizations. It sounds ominous, but its major contribution is to publish a yearbook of worldwide associations...from the boy scouts to labor unions.

Through the years the UIA has researched techniques for enabling interagency communication. I was in Brussels to speak with the Director General on the latest theories for meta-communication in my specific area of interest, worldwide school reform movements, and how they share information.

My wife, a junior high school science teacher, and my two daughters, 12 and 14, accompanied me on the trip. With the childrens' school principal's permission, we took the girls out of school for several months. Marian would provide instruction as the weeks rolled by.

We unpacked at the Brussels Hilton late one afternoon. The girls who were now getting a little travel weary and grumpy, said, "Let's have a hamburger for dinner tonight." The request seemed reasonable so at six o'clock we headed across the busy thoroughfare to a plain looking restaurant near the hotel. We checked the menu in the window, and saw nothing that might be a hamburger. I recommended that we keep walking until we found a hamburger restaurant.

Several blocks away we found another restaurant with a nice courtyard and attractive décor. We headed in. The eating rooms were on the second floor.

Quickly I reasoned we had made a serious mistake. The courtyard had a lovely fish tank with speckled trout swimming around. The maitre de wore a tuxedo, as did all the other waiters. We were the only guests in the place.

I explained that the girls would like a hamburger, and that Marian and I would eat off the menu.

" I am sorry, sir. We don't serve hamburgers here. May I suggest chateaubriand for four." I am sure that the girls had never heard the word "chateaubriand" before. They looked at me for an explanation.

"Sort of like a fine steak"

There was never a sign of agreement among the children. They were tired and hungry, and I was a bit embarrassed to leave. I said, "OK, medium rare."

We sat there eating bread and butter for what seemed a decade before dinner was served. The plates were placed with great care; an army of waiters delivered the meat and petite veggies with flourish. A silver gravey boat contained a luscious demi glace.

The food was wonderful; everything was done to perfection. But the girls ate with a sullen air of disgust. Their hamburger dinner had turned into a trial.

My trial was just beginning. When the check came it was for something between $200 and $250 dollars. I had about eighty dollars in my wallet. My watch would not be sufficient collateral…it was a cheap Timex. I explained to the maitre de that I had travelers checks at the hotel, but that I would leave my wife and daughters behind until I returned. I figured that they were worth at least $250.

I ran both ways to and from the hotel. The bill was settled with much calculation of exchange rates, size of the tip, and change from the travelers checks that I provided.

Meanwhile the girls just sat and stared at me like I was some sort of idiot. It was idiotic. I should have known what was in store when I saw the trout tank.

FOODS I NEVER ATE
AS A CHILD

I never ate a bagel until I was 45 years old. We ate white bread when I was at home as a child. Bagels were ethnic foods, and we didn't eat those.

We moved to Palo Alto, California about 1970 to work in the school district. We lived at the corner of Newell and Edgewood. Our neighborhood was disputing a plan to close the little concrete bridge into East Palo Alto adjacent to our property. The fancy-dancy Palo Alto folk wanted it closed so that the riff-raff could not enter. The bleeding hearts wanted it left open, as a token of welcoming all comers.

Beth and Keith Boyle invited the neighborhood to their home on a Sunday morning to discuss the matter. On arrival we were offered a glass of white wine and a huge tray of bagels with the usual cream cheese spread. With some hesitation I took a bagel and bit into it. It was delicious, and so began my love affair with bagels. From then on I would bike to the bagel store every Sunday morning and buy a bagful to last through the week. (When I returned home the bag would still be warm.) Now, thirty years later, we try to keep a few frozen bagels in the fridge. My favorite is an onion bagel. The "everything bagel" is overkill, as I try to sort out the various flavors.

As a child, anything green was suspicious, especially peas. Mother tried over and over to force feed me, resulting in more and more resistance.

Then when I was about five, Barney Ruckdershel had a birthday party at his house. It was a sit down luncheon; the entrée was chicken a la king, including a handful of peas. Torture. What to do? At home I would have shaken my head and asked for peanut butter. Here were my peers, and no mother to coddle me.

I inched up on a pea and ate it. It was NOT good.. So I pushed all the peas aside, and ate a few pieces of chicken. When Barney's mother said, "Are you done?" I handed her back the nearly full plate, relieved that the trauma would end.

From time to time Mother would buy peas in the shell, and I was delighted to shell them, but not eat them.

Who knows how old I was before I conquered my fear of peas. The date of my first happy pea escapes me, but now I love the taste of a fresh pea, boiled briefly and doused with butter and salt and pepper. Pea variants are OK too… peas with pearl onions, pea soup, or mashed peas with cream.

Fish is another category I didn't eat. I've documented the terrible salmon casserole mother concocted, and the household stench when it was baking. Nor was tuna salad on my list of acceptables. We were fishless at home. I never saw a fish filet darken our table.

Sometime on a weekend pass while I was in the army, the gang ordered shrimp cocktail, and I instructed the waiter to bring me one too. I watched the guys squeezing lemon juice on the shrimp dipping them into their red "cocktail sauce." It turns out that I loved the cocktail sauce, and forever think of shrimp as a spoon to eat the sauce with.

On a trip to England I ordered a shrimp cocktail, and it came with a mayonnaise sauce. How strange, I thought, they don't know how to present shrimp. Later I learned about tartar sauce and mayonnaise-based dressings.

As I matured, fish was presented to me at dinner parties, banquets, and during business travels. Eat it, or starve or be impolite. I learned that fish can be sauced like meats. Who knew? Some seafood was considered a treat, like Dover sole, and soft-shelled crab.

Once I attended a luncheon at the Maison Blanche (a fine restaurant opposite the Executive office building near the White House in Washington.) It is an elegant place where the elite meet to eat...but it is noisy, and the tables are close together. I heard someone at the table order an asparagus salad, and I told the waiter to bring me what she was having. When it came it was a white meat in a delicate white sauce, but no asparagus. The next day I called the lady and asked what we had eaten. "Swordfish", she responded.

I thought it was veal.

Now as an old man, I am not an adventurous eater. Give me meat loaf and a baked potato. Ketchup is a staple.

Meet Hugh
Missildine, Shrink

Meet Hugh Missildine, the psychiatrist for my boss's boss, Dave Cox. Dave needed a psychiatrist. He was a rats nest of neuroses. His petulant behavior caused his wife to become alcoholic. His sons were treated as underage recruits in the Marines. He treated employees as his minions. If he gave you an assignment, you were required to go to your desk, write up the assignment and return it to him with an estimate of when the job would be done.

Dave finally went to Hugh, the best family psychiatrist in Columbus, Ohio. Dave began to be softer, more sensitive to those around him. He decided to make Hugh part of our business family. Dave hired him half-time to write a monthly newsletter for pediatricians and general practicioners entitled, "Feelings and their medical significance." We also began a series of counseling booklets for parents about common pediatric problems: thumb sucking, colic, bed wetting, etc.

Hugh was a great addition to our medical staff. He began his medical career as a general practioner in Iowa. One day a young girl plunked down $.50 and said, "Tell me about sex." He realized that what most of his patients wanted was to talk about themselves, and he didn't feel prepared to help them adequately. After an army tour he went to Johns Hopkins for psychoanalysis and moved to Columbus, Ohio to start a practice. As Hugh tells it, he could get patients to talk about their deepest problems, but they were not getting well.

Then one day he had an amazing insight. We are all grown up children. We treat ourselves with the same attitudes as our parents had about us…we either accept those feelings or reject them. "I learned to listen to patients until I understood their child of the past, then I could become prescriptive." Patients started to get better faster. He quickly became the best known family psychiatrist in town.

At work, he began conceptualizing his newsletter, honing in on the family pathogens that messed up children: pathogens such as overindulgence, perfectionism, coercion. Each issue of "Feelings" would discuss a pathogen, illustrated with a case history, and include suggestions for working through the problem.

After a year we said, let's write a book, and Hugh agreed. Jim Jeffries, my boss, and I went to the Missildine home every Tuesday night for over a year. When we finished, we had a manuscript of 180 pages. The response from Simon and Schuster was, "Very good, now go write the book." Jim and I did not have much more to add so Hugh went to Harry Henderson, a writer at our ad agency and asked Harry to flesh out the book. It was published under the title, "Your Inner Child of the Past", and was very successful. Hugh split his first royalty check with Jim and me. My share was $30 dollars.

By now I was a vice president of the company, and Dave Cox believed that we all could benefit from some time on the couch. The sales manager went first, and I was next. I was unsure and curious whether or not I had any serious psychological problems. My Dad died when I as eleven, my brothers were drafted, and I became Mother's escort. I thought I might have an oedipal issue or two. And, basically I was afraid of Dave. When he exploded, which he did often, I became fearful for my job.

Hugh's first question was, "How do you feel inside your chest?" Over the next six months I explained my life story. I expected charges of at least $50 an hour. When the bills came, they were $15 an hour. I suspected that Dave was picking up the difference. Regarding my oedipal fears, Hugh concluded that I was fortunate because my relationship with my mother taught me to love women. Regarding Dave, Hugh hinted in a number of subtle ways that it was Dave who had the problems, not me. In six months, Hugh asked, what more needs to be done? I said that I needed to live with some new insights. I would be back if I needed more help. I did confront Dave whether he was paying for my therapy, and Dave said, "No."

Hugh was in great demand as a speaker in Columbus.…church groups, women's associations, service organizations. He told me that public speaking was very hard for him at first, but one night he threw away his cue cards, and just talked with the people, and it began to be a pleasurable experience. He solved problems by humanizing them. He opined that he was good at helping neurotics, but couldn't help psychotics very much. He took a few psychotic patients because he felt he should, but he had to nap after each session to get himself back on an even keel.

He was a character. He had a bad back, and as you passed his office he would often be flat on his back on the floor, whistling a happy tune. He taught us that grown men can be whimsical and even silly at times. Unfortunately, he was diagnosed as having bladder cancer, retired, and spent his dying days sculpting the heads of friends.

He was years ahead of transactional analysis, "I'm-OK-You're-OK" school of psychiatry. One other thing. His office had no couch. The patient sat in a chair next to his desk. I was disappointed that he didn't have a couch.

But what can you expect for $15 an hour?

Searching For The Muse
In London's West End

"HAIR" hit Broadway with rave reviews, celebrating the hippie culture. "Let the Sunshine In", "This is the Age of Aquarius" were smash song hits. Scandalous? At the end of the show the cast wiggled under a tarp and stripped naked, then came forward to the footlights.

After visiting friends in Scotland we decided to take the girls to see the show in London. They were preteens, and the show was the hottest ticket in town. It was a happy, lively show, and at the end when the cast stripped, the stage crew lit large searchlights facing the audience, blinding us from seeing any skin. Marian and I had never been to a rock concert. Our memory of the show was primarily the deafening sound flung at us from the stage.

In those days when you visited London, it was mandatory to see "The Mousetrap" by Agatha Christie. It had already run for over 24,000 performances. The play was first broadcast as a radio play in 1952 in honor of Queen Mary, wife of George V. At the end of each performance a spokesman asks the audience not to reveal the trick ending. Between acts we all predicted who we thought who had been the murderer. I was dead wrong. The murderer was _____.

Years later, visiting London with friends, we stayed at 11 Cadogan Gardens, one of those wonderful small boutique hotels noted for quality and fine service. We asked the concierge to get us some tickets for a Shakespeare play, and for a typical British music hall revue.

We went to the Shakespeare play with high expectations. It was a fiasco. The actors emoted as if paid extra for histrionics, and even then it was a dull, leaden performance. Half way through the play (no longer remembered) Marian lurched a little, stood up, walked to the side wall and stood there. When I got to her, she said she just wanted to sleep. We left the theater and put her to bed. She was not very responsive. (Recently, Marian had a MRI that revealed the scars of a stroke that had happened sometime in the past.) Thinking back on it, that is probably what happened that night. By morning she was responsive, and our trip continued.

I don't know what the concierge was thinking, but the "music hall" tickets he bought for us were for "Smokey Joe's Café", an American revue written by Lieber and Stoller, with 39 rhythm and blues and rock and roll songs. A British music hall revue it was not.

When in London we wanted to be entertained. We never went to serious theater. We saw "Phantom of the Opera" and the "Lion King." For sheer joy we saw, for the second time, "The Complete Works of William

Shakespeare in 90 Minutes" by the Reduced Shakespeare Company. The cast and comic play were superb.

As for nudity on stage, we had summer theater in Columbus, Ohio. The theater was a project of Sally Sexton, a rich, funny, eccentric woman. During each intermission she would make a little speech, welcome the audience, extol the next play, and make a few off-hand remarks. One night she said, "I have just returned from London where we saw "Oh Calcutta", the all nude one act plays by Kenneth Tynan. All I can say is that naked men should not run up and down stairs."

Nudity in the theater? Couldn't care less. But, is it art?

Response to Seeing "Hair" In London
by Janice Hudson

Being the ungrateful wretches my sister and I were, we were not thrilled about leaving school for two months to travel through Europe and Israel. Come on, I mean, like, our friends were much cooler, and like you know, your parents are SO uncool. Liz had a boyfriend, Randy, and I had this total crush on Mark. We didn't have much choice. So, off we went.

While we were in London, Mom and Dad took us to the theater several times, and we really liked it. Agatha Christie's "Mouse Trap" was really fun, and the history of the play meant something to me. Mark and I went to London five years ago, and saw it again. I'll give up the murderer for anyone interested for a large amount of money…but unfortunately the Mousetrap has run its course.

The night we went to see "Hair" Mom and Dad had a 'sitdown' with us at dinner before the show. " In this play, there is a scene in which everyone is nude. It's OK and we don't want you to be upset." We had seen nude people before. Well, we'd seen our parents nude, but whatever. My sister, Liz was eighteen months older and very sophisticated. At age 11, I wanted to be as cool as she was.

"HAIR" is a rock musical. After being dragged to a zillion cathedrals, art galleries, and museums, we were psyched. The play was glorious. Mom and Dad didn't like the loud rock, but Liz and I thought it was great. However, in the back of my mind, I was a bit apprehensive to see a bunch of nude people. Nudity had never bothered me, but these were strangers. The play was wonderful...loud rock music, beautiful songs, flashing lights, the works. When the nude scene happened, a tarp came up the cast stood proudly buck naked. It WAS a bit shocking. Not so much the women, but the men. I recall one slender actor right in front of me. He was, as they say, well endowed, and it grossed me out. The tableau only lasted a few seconds, and was over before I could take it all in. Afterword, I wondered what all the fuss was about. The nudity part was so short, it really didn't warrant the big build up.

We bought the cast recording, and Liz and I listened to it constantly. (I can still sing every song.) Mom and Dad's warning wasn't all that necessary. I'm pleased to report that I was not mentally scarred from seeing a bunch of hippies in the buff. As an adult in the medical profession, I have seen thousands of nude people, but they are not nearly as much fun as when they are singing in a rock musical. And that actor in front of me in the play...I hope he made some woman very happy.

TECHNOLOGY

In 1939, my father took the family to the New York World's Fair. One afternoon the five of us crowded into a darkened room at the RCA exhibit. The lights were dimmed, and we stared at a box with a window about 4 by 8 inches. The announcer boomed that we were about to see the future. The little window glowed, and we were looking at the crowd outside the building staring at a camera. The television era was upon us. In black and white.

Our fraternity, Phi Gamma Delta, sold magazine subscriptions so that we could buy a television set for the frat house living room. The little window in the box was still about 4 x 8 inches. Our regular sacred meetings were every Tuesday night in the attic. But no matter how much business was to be transacted, at ten minutes to eight the brothers became restless, and the meeting ended so we could race three stories down to the living room to see Milton Berle, and the Texaco Star Theater. The only other program we watched faithfully was "Kukla, Fran and Ollie" at supper time.

I am not a Neanderthal about technology, I am a Luddite, that is, I want to destroy it all. Radio is all I want, even though I never understood it either, or how air waves could transmit all that music to so many places at one time.

Today we are besieged with contraptions. We pay $39.99 a month for the privilege of carrying around a cell phone. That's nearly $500 a year. I estimate that I made at least 5 calls on the thing in 2009. You do the math. That's $100 a call.

We went to Radio Shack and bought a HD (high definition) radio so that we could have static free classical music. To achieve static free music you have to get the aerial just right. As soon as I do, the cat jumps up on the bookcase and wrecks the aerial arrangement. As if that were not enough, the radio has a wireless remote, so that we can turn the radio off or on from a distance.

We like to have a little music as we fall asleep. As we turn the lights off the radio is still playing. About one in the morning I wake, reach for the remote and turn off the radio….unless the remote has gone 180 degrees, in which case I turn on the static.

Remotes are all over the house. We have three ceiling fans, and they all have separate remotes enabling us to turn the fans on and off or low, medium and hi speeds. Another button on the fan remote enables the fan to change directions. Another button turns ceiling lights on and off, or to be dimmed.

We have remotes for the television set, and the DVD player. We love remotes so much that we never threw our old ones away, and have a basket full of them. It takes a genius to play a DVD on the Vizio television using two remotes. Marian wrote down the instructions carefully, but it doesn't work.

We are a computerized household. I have a beautiful iMac with a 27 inch screen. An honest analysis would find that I am using the computer many hours a day. But, I am not on Facebook. I don't Tweet. I don't text. I don't blog, and I have only Skyped twice. My old three–in–one printer was sluggish, noisy, had an inconvenient sloped top and too many buttons to push.. The small "digital window" was positioned where I could not see it. So I bought a new upscale one. It has had paper jams just like the old one.

We own a Kindle so I can instantly download books from Amazon averaging $9.99 per book. I've learned to change the size of the type, recharge the battery, order the New York Times Review of Books and scan several apps. (That is short for the word "applications" to the uninitiated.) BUT, I'm left with a sinking feeling that I am contributing to the demise of the book trade and the printed word. I do not enjoy reading with a sense of guilt.

My angst is considerably deeper. New things are constantly being introduced or improved. Should I have a smart phone, an ipod, an ipad, a laptop, a notebook and all those other engineering marvels? I'm speechless before the modern wireless era. Take it all back! I beg you. Maybe back to a singular Philco radio so I can listen to Amos and Andy weeknights and Jack Benny on Sunday evening.

Are they still broadcast? No, they are all dead.

ADMITTED CLOSET LUDDITE
BY JANICE HUDSON.

My Father recently wrote a Vin Yet he titled: "Technology". At 81 years old, I am constantly amazed at his level of sophistication with new gadgets. On his desk sits a sexy top of the line iMac that he plays like a Wurlitzer organ. He bought Kindle before most of the world knew what it was for. Despite Dad's tech savvy, neither he nor my mother can decode the mystery of cell phones. Every time I call them (when they have the phone on and charged), I hear "hello, hello. Marian, I can't get this thing to work", then silence. This was, at one point, a source of exasperation to me. We did tutorials, like "to answer a call, open it up. To end a call, close it.". I even set up speed dial. "OK, you guys, all you have to do is push '2' to call me, then the green button". At this point, I'm thinking their uncharged cell phone is in a drawer, dusty, uncharged and forgotten.

Cell phones are great. We can call our friends every 5 minutes to let them know of the thought of the moment, which they may or may not be interested in hearing. But, like anything, there are down sides. Recently I was out on a lovely trail with the somewhat hot-blooded Misu, my horse. My phone began to vibrate and beep, indicating an incoming text message. Ignore. Over the next 5 minutes, eight more texts came in. Like a good little phone slave, I finally pulled out the phone. All nine texts were from ATT giving me "tips". I have a tip: taking out my phone while riding my hot little chestnut mare on the trail is dangerous.

Despite this, we're hooked. One morning, while on my way to the barn, I realized I had left my cell phone on the counter. I panicked, driving nearly 25 minutes back to my house. Then the sudden clear epiphany. When did I, Janice Hudson, become so important? The answer is simple. I'm not. My whereabouts is not a matter of national security. When working as a nurse anesthetist, especially on call, I carried no less than three phones, sometimes four communication devices. A pager. A spectralink phone. A second spectralink phone if I was covering both OB and the house. And, of course my personal cell phone. I always wore a fanny pack with my emergency stuff, with all these phones and beepers attached. As I sauntered down the hall, they would make a 'kerchunk, kerchunk" sound, like an old time cowboy with his trusty revolver at his side. I hated them. Every time one or more devices rang, beeped, or vibrated it meant I had to go someplace to do something. Like putting in epidurals. Emergency surgeries. Codes. After a 24 hour shift, I tossed all the phones and pagers to the next staff nurse, feeling the freedom of no weight on my belt.

Our family has finally gone "all Apple, all the time". Apple's selling points? No unexpected crashes, great security, sexy design, and intuitive programs that are easy to use. My love affair with Apple, however, is quickly fading. Their programs, once so easy to use, are now just as complicated as a PC. Simple tasks become a search for an obscure "how to" buried deep within their website. The search for an answer often leads to page after page of unrelated material. Or, it's down in a techno language I don't understand. Frankly I don't want to understand it. New Apple products are sold without instruction books-"just go to the website!" Just how can I get to the freaking' website when my computer is down?

Then there is the proprietary Apple ware. Recently, I have tried to hook my computer to our television to watch streaming video-movies and such. In order to do so, I have already spent $80 for cables that the 'geniuses' assured me would work. To date, no go. I have, however, discovered a port of my television to plug into a PC. No muss, no fuss. 'PLUG IN HERE'. Have been wrestling with my laptop interface for 6 months. My newest can upload my music in a zillion ways with a PC. With my Apple, I can't upload music unless I- wait for it- buy a new proprietary cable that the Genius' "think might work". (See Genius discussion below)

One of my very dear friends is married to an engineer who works for Apple, and was an integral team member for the iPhones. The most hilarious part? She was given one of the new super spanky G4 iPhones- the project he has been working on for several years. To date she has not been able to set up her voice mail, and can't run many of the zillions of programs incorporated into said G4. When I ask him for help for a simple problem, he usually shrugs and says 'ask the genius bar guys, they know'.

Which takes us to the discussion regarding the Apple 'Genius Bar". For an additional chunk of money, you have free access to the Apple geniuses to solve any and all problems Apple. That, too, has become a bust. Took my laptop to them on several occasions only to have them scratch their heads, look doubtful, and proceed to erase my hard drive-not just on my computer, but my back up disc as well. That takes special talent.

There is no doubt that computers have changed the world forever. For the most part, all of this is a great thing. But in this author's mind- I'm considering going back to pen and paper. Anything that takes more than five minutes to learn just ain't worth it.

COMPUTERS ARE SUPPOSED TO MAKE OUR LIVES EASIER, RIGHT?
BY JANICE HUDSON

For the sake of brevity, I will attempt to boil this down without long explanations, or begin to rant. This is, again, why I am a closet Luddite.

For the past several months, we have been receiving enticing offers from a company we'll call, say, Atrocious Telephone Terrorists, offering high speed internet for a fraction of what we currently have on broadband. Since my husband and I are fiscally responsible, we thought we'd give it a try. We tried to cover all the bases.

"Is this fast enough to watch two different movies on two different computers?" I asked.

"Oh, no problem. You'd only see a difference if you were a high level gamer", the rep replied.

"We have iMac computers, does this cause any problems?" was my next question.

"Oh, no. We send you a router, and all you have to do is plug it in, and it WORKS!" she gushed on the other end of the phone.

"What if we have problems making it work?" I asked.

"We have both telephone and technical support available 24 hours a day", she replied. "We rarely see problems when people set up their systems".

Like an idiot, Mark and I bought it. We breathlessly waited for our new router to show up, to be followed by a technician to set it up the following day. We were assured that he or she could get our system up and running in no time.

Why, oh why did we fall for this?

On the appointed day, Jim, a very personable young man from the company showed up, wearing a big grin. "Welcome to ATT" he said. "You're going to love this. In the next 2 hours, he struggled to get the thing to work, but it seemed to finally happen. We were on line, and all that was left was to set up our new mailboxes.

Then, yes, you know the story, the trouble started. My laptop computer would not connect to the Internet. Mark's desktop would connect, but only intermittently. When he attempted to watch a movie on line, it spent at least 10 minutes buffering. Afterwards, the movie started, only to stop with an error message reading 'your Internet speed has changed. Please wait until we determine your speed so you will have no further interruptions'. Of course, 30 minutes later the rolling ball of death was still on the screen, with no evidence of any progress.

I called my good friend, Jim, back. "Jim, we're having trouble. We can't set up our mailboxes". He assured me all was well, and they would send over 'Gary', the top technical guru. I was quite clear:

1. We needed to get my computer on line and a mailbox set up.

2. Mark's computer was only intermittently on line and needed his mailbox set up. Prior to Gary the guru, Mark spent some 2 hours on the "tech line" with somebody in India who was unable to fix our problems. In addition, I spent some 6 hours trying to follow their on-line technical support to clear up the problem.

Gary, the guru, showed up around 6 PM. His first statement was "If you have a dog, you have to put it in another room". His second statement floored me.

"I cannot help you with any of your computer settings. ATT won't take responsibility if something happens to your computer."

"Gary", I said, somewhat testily, "the whole reason you are here is to set up our computers". After two hours, he ran a test on the router and assured us there was nothing wrong with the signal. His parting shot was "Janice, you need to take your computer to the Apple Store. Obviously it's a problem with your computer."

In the meantime, my health took a bit of a detour. I needed to be able to e-mail my physicians. We were trying to communicate several times a day. This required me to get on my husband's computer, log on to the ATT website in order to receive our mail. Often, the mail got misdirected, as our Guru, Gary, set up two different accounts- exfn, and exfn1. Nobody seemed to know which was which.

This went on for almost a week. Finally I told Mark I was done, and we were going back to our old Internet provider, despite the fact it was more expensive. He readily agreed.

The saga, as they say, continued. In order to unscrew our computers, we needed a new apple router to the tune of almost $200. Apple is known for simplicity in set up. This was, of course, not to be. After another day or two of following poorly worded instructions, we were no closer to having two functioning computers. Out of desperation, I happened to be at a local Radio Shack.

"Does anybody here know anything about Apple computers?" I begged, looking pathetic as possible.

Nathan, my now new hero, said he'd give it a shot. He came to the house, and within two hours had:

1. Both computers working

2. Both emails up and running

3. Set up our Blue Ray player to run movies and programs from the internet

And… fixed some problems with iPhoto that has plagued me for two years.

Lessons learned:

1. Atrocious Telephone Terrorists have not changed since they were known as "Ma Bell"

2. Never believe it when somebody tells you it's 'easy' to set up a complicated piece of equipment

3. Always read reviews of service before agreeing to change. When I returned to the Internet, I looked up this wonderful Internet service that ATT offered. Of course, as I suspected, there were nothing but hideous reviews with comments like ."DON'T EVEN THINK OF IT"

Minutiae

Our lives are dominated by little things, our minor compulsions that give life its routine and consistency. For example, what do I put in my pants pockets? For many years I put my wallet in the back wallet pocket. No longer. Now my wallet is in my right hand pants pocket. It shares that space with a small pocket knife. My right hand pocket has my car keys, some glucose tablets, our cell phone and a hanky. This order never changes. If I put my car keys in the left hand pocket I would be sure they were lost.

We have dozens of little ways to make our lives more comfortable. I have very dry skin, and I itch a lot. In response, I have three back scratchers located here and there…one by my computer, and one where I sit in the living room. Every once in a while an itch (most often on my ankle) will flair, and I am miserable. Therefore. I keep a tube of cortisone cream in my walker at all times. We buy cortisone in packs of four at Costco. I am never without it and I feel safer.

Our bedroom dresser has a normal order. Marian has allotted me one big drawer, and one small one. The small one contains my socks and the handkerchiefs. The large drawer, reading from right to left…underwear, T shirts, and then pajamas on the left. Don't mess with me. Do NOT change the order.

We have Kleenex arrayed conveniently all over the apartment, by our beds, by the computer, by Marian's living room chair. Your never know when your nose might drip or a sudden sneeze might arise.

Snacks are important, and a snack- attack can occur at any time, anywhere. But snacks should be healthy, not greasy or sweet. So we keep nuts around. Today I have cashews by my reading chair, peanuts by the computer, and almonds waiting by the stove. One handful is never enough, so two are always necessary. The only other alternative to a sudden hunger is pretzels. Not the puny kind, but those big, salt covered, hard beer pretzels I love. Marian asks, "Have you broken a tooth yet," "No, but I wouldn't be surprised."

Our small rituals give consistency to our lives. Yes, we can change, but it is painful to do so, particularly at our gentle age.

But other little things can be confounding.

When we moved to our current apartment, we had to find a self-cleaning electric cat litter box, not wider than 18 inches so that we could close the bathroom door. After weeks of searching we found and installed one. When we plugged it in I noted that it had a digital clock. I wonder whether cats can tell time. We never set the clock, so it always reads the wrong time of day. Poor cat.

Besides, cats can only read analog clocks.

THE MOST IMPORANT DECADE

Living eight decades is a long time, at least some people think so. Born in 1929, much water has gone over the dam, under the bridge and down the drain.

My first decade is a blur. I missed the depression. Dad was a newspaper reporter and had to commute from Philadelphia to New York to find work on an Italian newspaper. My strongest recollections of the 30s are of rainy days sitting under the card table with a sheet over it, pretending it was a tent and I was camping; of trips to Lancaster to see grandparents from both sides of the family; and of starting elementary school in Overbrook in West Philly. Mother had taught me to write my name, so I entered school directly into first grade...the youngest and shortest kid in line.

We can skip the 1940s, except that the Second World War was the major event. The war was believed to be a just war, and patriotism ruled the day and we won...my family never suffered in any way. My older twin brothers were drafted toward the end of the war, and were sent to Germany when the fighting was over. Dad died in 1942, and I became the man of the house. When Jack and Jim were discharged, the three of us went to college at the University of Pennsylvania, they to the Wharton Business School, and me to the College of Liberal Arts.

After graduation from college in 1950 I found work as a salesman with a small company in Columbus, Ohio. After three years in the army during the Korean war, I was sent to the home office to write and teach sales materials.

Soon after. I married Marian Brown, and we started a family…two daughters, Elizabeth and Janice. However, I was still not an adult, emotionally or intellectually. I was still learning my trade, pathetically other-directed, didn't have any worldviews to speak of, and I was terrified of my boss.

Then came the 60s, the most important decade of my eighty years. My immature innocence came face-to-face with momentous changes. Bob Dylan wrote two songs that disturbed, but were so true:

"Your sons and daughters
Are beyond your command
Your old road is
Rapidly agin'
Please get out of the new one
If you can't lend a hand
For the times they are a-changin'"

Bob Dylan
"The Times Are a Changin'"

"How many roads must a man walk down
Before you call him a man?
How many seas must a white dove sail
Before she sleeps in the sand?
Yes, how many times must the cannon balls fly
Before they're forever banned?
The answer my friend is blowin' in the wind
The answer is blowin' in the wind."

Bob Dylan
"Blowin' in the Wind"

The country, the culture and the society seemed to be disintegrating. John Kennedy, Martin Luther King and Bobby Kennedy were assassinated. (After the King murder, and the riots in Baltimore, we were traveling home from a vacation, stopped in Washington to see the Capitol. The place was ominously guarded by armed soldiers.)

The Vietnam antiwar movement was virulent and the current literature reflected the sentiment. "Catch 22" by Heller depicted the absurd craziness of war. Kurt Vonnegut wrote "Slaughterhouse Five," reporting the fire bombing of Dresden where 130,000 civilians were killed.

The civil rights movement bloomed. The tragedy of slavery and racial prejudice were exposed. Race riots threatened the peace in cities all over the country, often centered in the universities. Staid churches set up committees on Religion and Race, setting conservative members' teeth on edge. Black folks would no longer tolerate being treated as second class citizens.

The organized Church itself was experiencing a revolution. Ecumenism had already been introduced, so it was no longer necessary for Protestants to hate the Pope. Mixed marriages among Baptists and Methodists was no longer a sin. More critically, some Catholic priests in developing countries practiced Liberation Theology wherein priests became politically active in the hope of distributing more wealth to the poor.

Sexual freedom became a mainstay. Woodstock, that romp in the rain and mud occurred in 1969. Bumper stickers proclaimed, "If the van is a-rockin', don't come a-knocking." Something called "open marriage" permitting free exchange of sexual partners became avant-garde. The theater produced "HAIR" proclaiming "The Age of Aquarius."

Radical chic was described by Tom Wolfe in " The Electric Kool-Aid Acid Test." Leonard Bernstein had invited the Black Panthers to meet New York's hoi polloi.

Drug usage became common all over the country… not just pot, but LSD and other hallucinogenics. Cocaine dealers polluted the cities and made fortunes.

School systems came under fire. Education theorists in England proclaimed "the open classroom" to be the school of the future with team teaching, and each individual child carefully diagnosed so that they progressed according to their individual needs. Learning by rote came under scrutiny in favor of affective learning, relying on students' emotional needs. Ivan Illich, headquartered in Cuernavaca, Mexico called for "Deschooling Society."

Each of these movements had an impact on me. My worldview became very liberal socially, but my personal fiscal beliefs remained conservative, favoring limited government. At work I was promoted to Vice President of Sales Promotion and Advertising, and I became active in the community, becoming Chairman of the Urban Education Coalition, hosting a weekly radio program on education, and challenging the school system to release test scores before approving a bond issue. In time I resigned from work to join a university-federal consortium program entitled, The National Program for Educational Leadership. As part of that experience Marian and I took the children out of junior high school for three months to tour school systems in England and Israel before taking a job in Palo Alto to head a long range planning project entitled, Project Redesign.

Half way through the project, the school board hired a new superintendent who wanted his own staff. We finished the project with dozens of recommendations, but even though we had a board member from Hewlett Packard, our suggestions neglected to note the emerging role of technology (computers) in educational procedures. As Project Redesign came to a close I was asked to return to the company I had left to help deal with social critics planning a boycott against Nestle for selling infant formula in developing countries.

My time in the public sector was instructive and helped me grow, but as a "change agent", I was not too successful. School systems are so rigid and inflexible because of state curriculum law, nervous teachers' unions and local traditions. Schools are very hard institutions in which to make dramatic changes. Putting one adult in a room with thirty kids demands a lot of structure, skill and discipline.

Every decade has its own highlights, but nothing like the impact of the turbulent, disruptive 60s. Those events changed my life, but in a good way. I became a wiser, more experienced, competent adult. At least I thought so.

Burglary

We live in a world where burglary is common. Most people have experienced some form of theft...purse snatching, house burglary, a disappearing camera at the beach, etc. Some burglaries are minor, and some touch our lives in significant ways. Some folks even approve of robbery...take the Gideons for example. Every motel room in America has a Gideon bible in the telephone drawer. I suspect that they are delighted every time one is purloined. Another soul might be saved. That is the definition of wishful thinking.

We owned a 90 acre farm in rural Ohio as a weekend retreat. The house was at the end if a long 1/4 mile lane. We felt secure because two cars could not pass on the lane, and a burglar would never know whether we would be coming or going. The farm house contained a few nice antiques we had acquired at country auctions, but mostly castoffs, but nothing of great value. Nevertheless we were burglarized. Apparently someone was setting up housekeeping. They took our bed, sheets, blankets, towels, pots and pans, and a mixture of other items that implied they were setting up housekeeping. The burglars even took a framed, reproduction of a Chagall print and an old Jerome mantel clock.

Several months later we had dinner at a restaurant several miles to the north. The restaurant had a small antique shop in a separate building. We always scanned the merchandise before going home. We found our Jerome clock. We knew it was our clock because a small piece of veneer had fallen off, and I had pasted it back on amateurishly. The repair job definitely identified the clock. I informed the shopkeeper, only to be told that the clock was on consignment from someone living at Buckeye Lake, several miles to the south. I notified the police, and was told they could do nothing because it was in a different jurisdiction.

Some years later we built a new home on the property. I designed it myself, and made a few architectural errors. I forgot to include a front door, and found that in Ohio winters we needed a garage, so we set upon a redesign project to make the house more livable. We used local contractors to whom we gave keys and the code to turn off the alarm system. Over the months of construction we had dozens of unknown workers there while we were working in Columbus.

My mother died, and while we were at the funeral the house was burgled. This time it was serious. These burglars were professionals, and focused on Marian's jewelry. Through the years I had a number of fine pieces designed and custom made for her. All gone, even the pearls that she wore at our wedding. I had acquired some fine garnet jewelry in Germany when I was stationed there. All gone. I had a silver box of watches and cufflinks in my dresser. They took my Rolex, but threw the Timex on the floor. Nothing was ever recovered. We settled with the insurance company for about $8000, but we never again bought valuable jewelry.

Several years later, we returned from work to find the front door wide open and CDs scattered all over the front steps. This time the burglary was of a different ilk. Sliding glass doors were kicked in, and the house trashed. Clearly not a professional break in. Probably it was a gang of young people doing damage for the hell of it. Not much of value was taken. Liquor, drawers pulled out and dumped on the floor, footprints on walls and doors where they had kicked. Toilet seats ripped off, etc. My friend's weekend home up the hill was also trashed, broken glass everywhere, and in his case, tennis rackets and liquor stolen. Several weeks later we received a call from the sheriff in Newark, Ohio. They had stopped a car for a traffic violation, and in the trunk found a roll of pennies that Marian had made. She had put our name and address on the roll. The stolen tennis racket was there too, and some of the missing liquor. We never were told what happened to the burglars, their ages, or the outcome of the arrest.

We suspect that they were teenagers looking for liquor, got drunk, and the burglary got out of hand. I recall an incident in my youth when my older brothers got into similar trouble. Their high school fraternity rented a house in Ocean City for a week on the Jersey shore. The kids drank too much beer and trashed the house. They tore out the stair railing. slit the pillows and dusted the house with feathers, smashed the dishes, and made a complete mess of the house. My Dad received a telephone call saying that the gang was in jail, and would require an adult to bail them out. Dad and I drove to Ocean City, and there they were in a cell with several of their buddies. They seemed unperturbed, happy, and singing, " If I Had the Wings of an Angel." Ultimately the group only had to pay for cleanup and repair.

We were told that our jewelry burglars had a specific MO. (Modus Operandi). They were known to the police as the "pillowcase burglars." On entering a home they would steal a pillow case, and fill it with valuable small things before leaving, seemingly knowing exactly what they were looking for.

The person or persons burglarizing our farm of the bed and blankets never upset us. I hoped they would be happy, and raise a trailer full of kids.

SEND IN THE CLOWNS

The cliché proposes, "Washington is broke." It is, and there are many reasons for it. To begin with, 34,700 registered lobbyists ply their trade in Washington…lobbyists on the right, the left, for corporations, for labor unions, for environmentalists, for everything. In addition, the city has about an equal number of lawyers who are not registered as lobbyists, but aid in lobbying for clients. We have 100 senators and 435 House members. Do the math. Every issue considered brings a wave of lobbyists to the hill all pleading their side of the question. And they come with checkbooks.

While many criticize "corporations" for buying Washington, the senators and representatives themselves seek the money. I worked for a division of Abbott Laboratories. The phone rang daily in the office with a hill staff member reminding us that the fundraiser would be tomorrow night, and a table of ten would cost $10,000. On average, the Abbott lobbyists would go to two fundraisers before going home for dinner. It was important to spread the money around…to both

Republicans and Democrats. Sooner or later both sides would have their turn in charge.

My experience confirmed that our money would not guarantee a vote for our position. But it would guarantee a hearing, an appointment...usually with a senior staff member. Think of it. Thousands of lobbyists roam the halls of Congress daily. Congressional staffs remain friendly, usually with the question, "What do you want?" or "Do you know an easy way to fix it?"

These days negative tensions and gridlock are high between the Democrats and Republicans. Each news cycle brings new examples of bad blood among the parties. How did that come about? I'm old enough to remember friendships between Everett Dirkson and Hubert Humphries trading barbs but shaping compromises to pass bills. Daniel Moynihan was a brilliant centrist helping the Congress do good things.

And then conservative Robert Bork was nominated to the Supreme Court by Ronald Reagan. A partisan war broke out. Ted Kennedy led the charge. He arranged a massive PR campaign, direct mail, hostile press releases, all outside the hearings themselves. The Republicans were startled, and very angry. From that time both parties began to play dirty, which continues to this day, poisoning and compounding the legislative process.

I love politics. My Dad was the political editor of the Philadelphia Evening Ledger. He covered Pennsylvania legislature, and every four years the presidential conventions and elections. (A family legend claims that Dad wrote Wendell Willkie's "One World" speech in 1940, but I have no proof of the story.)

On election nights the family sat around our Philco radio tallying votes from around the nation. Dad's newspaper, The Evening Ledger was Republican, but Dad's father had been the Democratic state chairman in Pennsylvania. The result is that I am very liberal socially, and conservative fiscally.

I am deeply troubled. The government has become too big, too complex, too controlling. We are good at adding new bureaus and regulations, but terrible at cleaning out the attic from time to time. Bureaucracies become bloated and inefficient, and change seems impossible. Somehow we think that if it is government-run it is efficient and useful. What folly.

Early in the 80s a seminal book entitled, "Friendly Fascism" was published. The premise is that we are rapidly becoming a nanny state with the government and other power elites believing that they know what is best for the general population. "You will wear seat belts; you will not eat French fries; you will not drink soft drinks; you will not study embryonic stem cells; you will wear helmets if you drive a motorcycle." The list is endless. The government doesn't say, "we recommend". Congress passes a law so that if you don't comply, you are a criminal. (Fortunately most laws are not enforced once they are enacted.)

Washington spends money like a drunken sailor. Dirksen said, "A million here, and a million there, and you are soon talking about real money." Now we say a billion here and a billion there, and soon we are talking about real money. The Republicans had their chance and failed to quell rampant spending. They loved earmarks too much. The Democrats have gone for broke…literally. When I write to Senator Dianne Feinstein to express my concern, I receive a boilerplate form response in three weeks. Senator Barbara Boxer does not reveal her e-mail address. Apparently she knows best what I think and need. The sausage factory grinds on.

Where is the political Moses we need to lead us out of the wilderness to the promised land? I am pissed and frustrated, but I am too old and crotchety to go to a Tea Party rally.

Summer Jobs

When a teenager enters high school he and his family begin to think it is time for him (or her) to get a job during the summer months. It is a rite of passage...getting a social security number, having a little of your own money in your pocket, and the feeling of being grown up. Of course, you planned to save all the earnings for the following school year, but it was too temping not to buy something immediately with the first check...and the second check, and the third.

THE DOG HOSPITAL

I once described working in the office of veterinarian Doctor Otto Stader. I had the exciting job of cleaning the soiled dog cages in the morning, mixing and baking the next day's food, combing and bathing those dogs who needed grooming, and watching Dr. Stader do dozens of spaying operations. After two months I loathed cocker spaniels who bit me regularly. I decided that cleaning soiled dog cages was not an occupation I coveted.

THE GOLF DRIVING RANGE

One summer my brothers, Jack and Jim, with two of their buddies took over the management of a golf driving range in King of Prussia, PA. The range had a small food stand by the parking lot where golfers could get cold drinks, hot dogs, hamburgers and ice cream. My summer job was to man the stand while my brothers retrieved the balls from the range.

It was a small operation, and we did not have one of those tractors that ran back and forth collecting balls. Instead, we jerry built a large piece of plywood with some straps so that the pick-up could be done, even when the golfers were practicing their drives. Golfers took great pleasure in aiming for the plywood, screaming "Got One" when the plywood was struck.

The only trouble was that the driving range did not produce any income. The reason…we ate all the profits. Jack and Jim loved milk shakes and made dozens of them. When their friends stopped by they would provide a round of hamburgers, potato chips and a Coke for every one. Profits those days…nil.

I think my salary was $10 per week, and all the food I could eat. Fair enough.!

SELLING CHRISTMAS TREES

Although not a summer job, at Xmas time we sold Xmas trees in front of a local grocery store. The twins and their friends, Bud Jackson and Jack Muntz would drive down to the Philadelphia railroad yards and select "bundles" of trees for $10 each. The number of trees in a bundle varied from one to six trees. The one-tree-bundle would contain one tree, 10 feet tall, where as the six-tree-bundle would have six 4 foot trees.

A bundle sometimes contained a misshapen tree. That was OK. We would carefully explain to the customer that the tree was especially grown to fit in a corner, or against a wall. (Surprising how many buyers bought into the scam, and left happy with a god-awful looking tree.)

When a tree sold, I sawed off the tree trunk bottom flush, and nailed on a green wooden stand, hoping that it would stand straight when set upright.

The operation was profitable. We couldn't eat trees, so each partner made a stunning $100 during the season.

THE ROAD GANG

Perhaps the most unlikely summer job I ever had was the summer I worked on a road gang. I was awarded the job through a political connection where we lived. Each morning the boss would pick up the gang in an open-bed truck and take us to the work site. We installed a guardrail along the narrow road adjacent to the Schuylkill river. My work tools were a long handled shovel and an eight-foot pointed steel bar for wedging out rocks. The post holes we dug were to be six feet deep for the posts. At the time I weighed 125 pounds, a 125 pound weakling. The holes I dug usually had a boulder at the five foot level, and I struggled to extract rocks out of the hole.

The remote road was famous for having a rock outcropping at ten feet above and slightly over the pavement. The boss decided we had to cut back the rock so that big trucks could drive safely by. He ordered jackhammers for the task. Joe was the only person who had the strength to lift the hammer up to work on the stone. During a break they asked me whether I would like to see what a jackhammer felt like in action. I had trouble lifting the heavy tool to the upright position. When I squeezed the trigger it jumped all over the place, and my toe hollered , "LOOK OUT you fool."

BUSSING TRAYS AT A HOTEL NEAR BOSTON

In the summer of 1949 a fraternity brother and I sent resumes to resort hotels all over the East coast. We chose the Hotel Preston in Swampscott, Massachusetts because they offered free lodging, a decent salary and a scenic, cliff side setting on the Atlantic. The Preston catered to a wealthy clientele from Boston. Many of the guests came year after year, and the atmosphere was casual and friendly. The help were encouraged to mingle with the guests. At the Thursday night dances, the young male employees asked the dressed-to-kill old ladies for a dance.

Fred and I worked in the dining room, bussing trays. Most of the waitresses were part of the permanent staff who traveled to West Palm Beach in the winter, and to Swampscott in the summer. They didn't fraternize with the college kids. They, not we, received all tips.

Dinner was served in one sitting. At 7 PM the dining room doors were opened, and all the diners came in at once. The three-course meal was served efficiently while a house band played dinner music.

Life was serene except for one problem. We were housed in a barracks, four to a room. One of our roommates, Bob, a medical student from Toronto, hated to get up in the morning. When we woke him, he would wake up snarling and swinging his arms like a boxer. He was dangerous, even though he had a gentle temperament when fully awake. We had to be up and dressed early to serve breakfast. So, we set up a schedule to wake Bob so that each roommate had only two days a week to put his life in danger.

WORK BECOMES REAL

The summer I worked on the road gang I took Hammond organ lessons at night so that eventually I could work my way through college playing the organ in bars and roller skating rinks.

When I played for the skaters I used a metronome. If you messed up a rhythm, you might have 200 skaters falling on the floor. It was so boring that I had fun by playing the music backwards every once in a while.

Nobody ever noticed.

WHALE WATCHING...
THAR SHE BLOWS

Jean Martinez said that watching a sailboat race is like watching grass grow. Even with binoculars the thrill of a sailboat race never seems exciting from a distance. There is another sport that has a similar feel about it: whale watching.

Many years ago, in the early 70s, we took a good bottle of wine and a carload of friends to Point Reyes, California to watch the whales swim South. We climbed high on a bluff, broke out the cheese and wine and waited, and waited, and waited, It was a beautiful day, blue skies, fresh wind, and a beautiful view of the ocean and whitecaps. Then someone screamed, "Water spout!" It took a moment to get the binoculars focused, and then, nothing. We had missed that all-important spout. Before the day was over we had all seen a spout, or thought we did, and that was good enough. We could report that we had been whale watching.

Then came two cruises to Alaska's Inside Passage on Cruise West. They promised whale sighting, and we had many. Spouts galore. On one occasion they stopped the boat and dropped an underwater microphone so that we could hear the whales talk to one another. What did we hear? Nothing. Not a peep. Apparently we had found a pod of dumb whales who never learned to talk. The following day we saw a pod of Orcas, sometimes called killer whales. They swam through the water with their dorsal fins looking more like sharks at the surface. They didn't talk either.

While waiting to see the next whale, the loud speaker announced that we would soon be passing an "island" of sea otters playing in the surf. It was true. We passed by perhaps eighty five otters swimming on their backs, and occasionally diving, presumably to look for dinner. We oohed and aahed at their cuteness. I could imagine a hungry orca having a riotous supper.

"Look hearty, mates. Half a mile to starboard…all the otter you can eat."

On the Alaska cruise through Glacier Bay we did see a whale breach, twist out of the water, looking just like that insurance commercial.

Whale watching continued when we went to Nova Scotia for a circle tour in a 32 foot RV. (I wanted to find out if buying an RV, and traveling around the country all year was a good retirement strategy. It is not. That damned RV was like a noose around our neck. Finding a parking spot in the center of a small village was a nightmare.)

One port town in Nova Scotia announced a day of whale watching, and Marian and I decided to do it. Travel friends, Donn and Sharon stayed ashore because Sharon gets seasick easily. How wise they were.

It was a very windy day, and the swells were sizable, with a dash of whitecaps making unending spray. The boat was seaworthy, but not by much. We lunged and jerked hither and yon, getting colder and colder by the hour. No whales in sight for a very long time. The captain was persistent. He would not return to shore until he had displayed a whale. He would slow the boat to a stop, examine the horizon, until he hollered, "There's one." Then he would lunge ahead full throttle toward the spout, the boat banging up and down, mostly out of the water. Late in the afternoon we saw several spouts at a distance, but no bodies. Finally the horror was over, and we headed to shore, cold, wet, and not caring if we ever chased a whale again.

Marian says she wants to go to Baja in the winter to see the baby whale calves. I'll go, but I have conditions. They must wheel me in a wheelchair to an ambulance who will drive us to the pier in San Francisco. (No airplanes to see baby whales.) I will rest in a comfortable stateroom napping and reading all day, and will not take any shore tours to buy trinkets in Mexico. If Marian wants to take a day trip in a rubber raft for a close up view, that's OK by me, as I contemplate supper and our wine choice. Back in San Francisco, we will reverse the process, and I will be hand delivered to my cozy abode in assisted living, none the worse for wear so that I can watch the baby whales on PBS.

If you want a really spectacular and exciting vacation, let me tell you about glacier watching.

OPRYLAND UNDER WATER

May, 2010. The Opryland Hotel is under water, as is the Grand Ole Opry. The hotel was first conceived by a group of musicians, and included comedian Minnie Pearl. They invested their money in a huge hotel near the Opry so that visitors would have a world class place to sleep.

"World class" is in the eye of the beholder.

Once in the '80s, we stopped there on the way home from Florida at the end of January. I was having some back problems at the time, and walked with some pain, supported by a cane. An Ohio neighbor, Norm McCray, flew to Florida to drive us home.

We turned off the superhighway and had our first glimpse of the hotel. It was gigantic, four or five wings emanating from a central hub. We pulled into the entry garage, were handed a number, and directed to the lobby. The attendant would retrieve our luggage, and we would pick it up after we checked in.

I have some hearing lapses, and the clerk at the desk spoke in a thick French accent. The lobby music boomed, and I could not hear what she was saying. They found our reservations, signed us in, and handed us a brochure and a map. Our bellboy walked us to the luggage shed where we picked out our bags from among hundreds sitting there. He then started the long walk to our rooms. He explained that the hotel was built over time, and that the levels did not match. To get to the second floor in one building would require going to the third floor in an adjacent building. It was very confusing, and my back was aching.

At supper time we decided to go to the food court where we would not need dinner reservations. We started on the long trek that, without exaggeration, was a quarter mile away. When we finally arrived a sign informed us that the food court was closed that night, and would open in the morning. Now what?

The hotel had six or seven restaurants. We just kept walking until we encountered the first. "Do you have reservations?" "No." "We are sorry but we are completely booked." Marian stepped forward. " My husband is diabetic, and we need to eat. Do you have some crackers, or some bread to tide him over." "No Ma'am, we are completely booked." I thought Marian would kill the guy. She lurched forward, and Norm grabbed her before she could do harm.

Now what? Norm said he would find a wheel chair and be back to take us to the next restaurant. When he returned we discovered that the wheel chair was defective, and scrapped along the tiled hallway. The next restaurant we encountered did not require a reservation and we were eventually seated, and served. The waitress explained that she worked at the hotel for five years, and still got lost on occasion.

Following dinner we decided to take the boat ride through the ground floor lobby that soared 90 or 100 feet to the glazed roof. (It was like a jungle in there.) We found the boat dock, and they explained that our wheel chair would be to the left as we exited the boat that wended its way through the fake waterfalls, forests, and impressive light show. We exited the boat, and the wheel chair was there. We pushed ahead to an elevator that had only two buttons…first and second floors. We pushed the button to the second floor (the actual lobby level), and we got out to a closed cul-de-sac with a balcony overlooking the place we wanted to be. After going back down we found our way out and eventually made our way back to our rooms. I inserted our plastic card in the lock, and the door would not open. Marian tried, Norm tried, both with no luck. Norm went to his room, called the desk, and a bellhop finally appeared to open our door. I was fuming. When we got up in the morning I declared that I wouldn't spend another hour in this horrible place. We went to the garage and left immediately.

We had a wonderful sausage McMuffin (with egg) at the nearest McDonalds. Thank God for greasy fast food…no reservations needed.

LEARNING TO LOSE BETS: TWO YEARS IN A ROW

Keith Boyle was a painting professor at Stanford. His wife Beth was completing her law study. They were a delightful couple who lived directly across the street when we lived in Palo Alto. After moving back to Ohio, we stayed in touch.

Among other things, Keith was interested in the Super Bowl games, and we decided to make a bet. If I won, he would give me one of his colorful prints. If he won, we would take them to one of the finest restaurants in the nation. I lost.

Business travel had taken me to the North Shore, north of Chicago, where I learned about "Le Francaise" then considered one of the top ten restaurants in America, and we made plans for the dinner. The reservations were made months in advance. The Boyles flew to Chicago at their expense, and off we went to dinner. I determined that we would spare no expense.

"Le Francaise" was housed in a one story building with all of the usual French-country décor in a small rural Illinois town. When presented the menu I said we wanted an appetizer, a salad, a fish course, a meat course and dessert. If we wanted a soufflé, it had to be ordered before the meal, which we did. I told the waiter to pick the wine after we ordered. I can no longer remember what each of us ordered for dinner, but can remember the wine, a San Michelle chardonnay from Oregon. (It pleased me that our waiter didn't choose an over-priced wine from their selection.)

Before the meat course, the staff rolled out a trolley with the various meat cuts displayed so that we could pick our bloody hunk. I use the word "staff" because by now we had an army of waiters serving us. As each course was served, a gang of four would surround the table with plates covered with silver domes, and at the proper moment the domes would be whipped off with great fanfare. By the time the soufflé arrived I was stuffed to the gills. The waiters poked a hole in the soufflé, poured something in, and the whole thing gushed a raspberry sauce like a volcano. The meal was a success. It only cost me a little over $400, before the 20% tip.

But my bad luck was not over yet. The following year we made the same Super Bowl bet. This year my loss would produce four tickets to "Lena Horne: The Lady and Her Music" the one-woman show appearing on Broadway to rave reviews.

On the appointed weekend, the Boyles flew from California, and Marian and I flew from Ohio. The show was wonderful. In the first half Horne sang her signature song, "Stormy Weather" to a grateful audience. But, the last song of the evening was "Stormy Weather" again, this time with passionate emotion. "Don't know why… there's no sun up in the sky… stormy weather." Every word had meaning. The ovation was thunderous.

There is a moral to this tale: Keith knew what he was betting on. I did not. NEVER BET WHEN YOU KNOW YOU ARE GOING TO LOSE… unless you want to.

The Ring:
Lost And Found

A few days ago I looked down, and noticed that the ring on my right hand that I had worn since 1953 was missing. I never take it off, so it was a puzzle.

In 1953 I was stationed in Bad Nauheim, Germany, 25 miles north of Frankfurt. I was billeted in a residential hotel called the Kaiserhof. The town is a famous spa town going back into the 1800s with a marvelous array of art noveau buildings housing the sprudel (or baths).

Adjacent to the baths were parks, restaurants, boutiques of every sort, bakeries, the post office, churches, railway station and private health clinics. My operational post was five miles away in Butzbach, and I spent hours in quaint Bad Nauheim wandering about listening to band concerts, eating in restaurants and window shopping in the stores.

The war had been over for six years, and an air of normalcy pervaded the place. Soldiers were still required to wear uniforms, but remnants of a war economy still existed. For example, I bought a wonderful Grundig radio with my cigarette allotment so that I could have music in my room. I sent home a Rosenthal dinner service for twelve, and some beautiful fragile glass tablewear. (I was one of the few bachelors with a hope chest.)

When I was eleven or twelve, mother bought me a gold signet ring for Christmas. When I played the piano, I would take the ring off so it would not click on the keys. In time the ring disappeared.

So I decided I wanted to buy another ring to replace my long lost one. Wandering through the jewelry stores in Bad Nauheim, I finally settled on a bloodstone ring in a gold setting that I have worn for fifty seven years.

As my weight increased, the ring got tighter and tighter. It became necessary to resize the ring. The jeweler said the ring had worn so thin that a safe resizing was not possible. He recommended a new gold setting which we ordered. The new ring was a bit more fanciful than the original ring, but it had one problem. The stone fell out, and I discovered it on the floor of our apartment. They glued the stone back in, and in a week, the stone fell out again. This time the jeweler recommended that he put small gold prongs over the stone as protection. Now the problem is that the prongs snag on cloth, and I fear ripping a prong off every time it happens.

The stone has remained in place.

Later I woke, and the ring was gone. Weight loss had made the ring too large, and it was loose. We searched hallways, the lost and found, and various wastepaper baskets that I had thrown things into. The next morning Marian found the ring on the floor by my side of the bed.

The ring mystery, however, has triggered a flood of memories about my tour of duty in Bad Nauheim Germany in 1953. I logged onto the internet, and found a picture of the hotel where I lived and the famous spa down the street. But I have not been able to find a picture of the street where I bought my ring.

Ah, sweet mysteries of life. Things lost are found. Things found are lost. Life goes on.

YES, YOU CAN GO BACK AGAIN: SOUVENIRS

One summer we drove to Florida. Mother bought a purple chenille bedspread from a roadside stand in Georgia. It was my bedspread for years. When the family drove to Maine the next summer and visited the Desert of Maine, we bought a small display of colored sand in a glass tube. I also remember a 10" tall totem pole from an Indian site somewhere. These small gifts would often remain in our bedrooms over the summer, and usually disappear during the school year.

When I started to travel as an adult I still had a desire to buy a small token of the trip to savor when I got home, like the small bronze head of Buddha that I bought in Geneva. It sits on a small table next to my computer. It is obviously a fake reproduction, but it pleases me to remember the rainy night when I spotted it in a darkened shop. (I know it is a fake because I saw another just like it in a nearby shop.) Sitting on the same small table is a small ceramic oil lamp I bought in Amsterdam on a very cold, rainy Sunday afternoon as I wandered the streets. The small golden round lamp has a word incised in the clay…Om, the Hindu word meaning God. At home in Ohio, I would light the lamp when guests came as symbol of welcome.

Nostalgia has its roots in ego. Our little souvenirs, carefully packed in dirty laundry in our return-home luggage, reminds us of an experience someplace we had been, or a pleasant experience on a vacation. To my left, I note a larger than life blue plastic frog from Sanibel, Florida. The frog reminds me that it is from a store next to the restaurant, THE TIMBERS, where one night we ordered a vodka martini with a twist. The drink was gigantic, served in a water glass. When it came, Marian didn't touch hers. She thought it was her ice water.

In an antique shop in Tel Aviv, we bought a group of Luristan knives and a small axe said to be 3000 years old. Later, I found one matching ours in the Persian display at the British Museum, and I began to believe that ours might be real, even though I know that they are more likely reproductions, based on the bargain price we paid. Craftsmen have learned to bury newly made objects for a year or so, giving them that ancient look. We want to be fooled.

One dreary winter we spent six weeks at Sea Ranch on the Mendicino coast wondering whether we should retire there. Route One washed out north and south of our site, requiring us to get back to civilization by driving up to the top of the mountain, and taking the ridge road south. Half way we passed a glass blowers shop in a remote no man's land. We stopped, and bought a lovely orange and blue bowl. The next year we bought a small vase. Both glass objects have survived three downsizings. The glass blower incised our names on the bottom of the bowl, but he spelled Marian's name incorrectly, but that is not a terrible crime, nor does it decrease our enjoyment of the colorful bowl.

Fifty years ago, people sent post cards from remote spots. After returning home they were often arrayed in scrapbooks as reminders of the trip. (Whatever happened to scrapbooks?)

When wealthy young Europeans were sent on the "grand tour" it was usually intended to be an educational tour to learn about art, and a shopping trip to bring home tapestries, cameos, sculpture, and paintings. Venice was always on their tour, and Murano chandeliers grace many an English estate. When Ohioans drive to Florida, they always return with oranges and marmalade from roadside stands.

Returning from a tour of duty in Germany, my brothers bought me a fine multifunction wristwatch with self-winding, date, moon phases, a timer and other do-dads I can't remember. I was 15 years old. The watch was a wonderful souvenir, and I could not resist prying off the back cover to examine and tinker with the works. The watch lasted one month before it was frozen and worthless.

Sometimes souvenirs lose their identities. On that little table next to my current computer is a tasteful little ceramic bowl in which I keep a heap of Hershey's Kisses. We have had several of these bowls around the house for years. But I have no idea when and where we bought them. They have lost their identity as a souvenir. Now I can enjoy them without any memory, and enjoy them for the chocolate, and their tasteful form and color.

As Freud said, sometimes a cigar is just a cigar.

ARE YOU A GOOD SWIMMER?

My wife knows how to swim. Both of my daughters learned how to swim. Elizabeth swam for a while with her high school team. But I can't. I have to fake swimming. No one ever taught me. I know what it looks like. Head in the water, head to the side to gulp air. All rhythmic and beautiful. Me: I gasp and gasp, roll over on my back and float until I can breathe again.

My first encounter with expansive water was at my grandfather's summer home in York County, Pennsylvania, along the Susquehanna River near York. His 400 acre summer home abutted the river although the house was far from the water. He had a road bulldozed to the bluff above the river...but we never went there. The bluff was too steep. Rather, the family would drive us several miles down the road, through the woods on a one lane dirt road, to park in front of a turn-of-the-century rundown white frame store where you could by pop, ice cream, some dry goods, and BAIT, mostly worms in a can, or minnows. We would already be in our bathing suits for splashing, and we always bought a can of worms for part two of the excursion. (The summer home had a corner stacked with fishing rods, reels and hooks.)

Fishing rods in hand, we would descend a long flight of rickety wood stairs to the water's edge, near a small float. The river was very wide at the location, and I don't remember any current. My brothers and I would splash around the float in four foot water until we tired, and then on to fishing. We never caught anything, but it didn't matter. The trip ended with a popsicle or an ice cream cone.

We never actually swam. Nor did Mother and Dad swim.

At home in Philadelphia, the nearest swimming pool was a few miles south of Haverford Avenue and City Line, called Llanarch. Neighbors would take turns driving a bunch of kids there for the day. Bag lunches were packed (a peanut butter sandwich with a banana, and a candy bar). The adults were adamant that we could not go into the water until an hour after we ate. If you did, they said we would have a cramp and drown.

We splashed around for hours, but never went into "deep water". We would jump off the edge in water where we could stand up, grab the edge of the pool, and pretend we were swimming.

Fast forward to college days. To graduate from the University of Pennsylvania you had to know how to "swim" four lengths of the college pool. Whoops! I did want to graduate, so in I plunged, and failed. I was then enrolled in the swimming program for a semester. When the instructor greeted us, he outlined the course.

To graduate, we had to cover four lengths of the pool without assistance, and know how to dive off the low and high diving boards head first. And, no bathing suits were permitted in the pool. That last bothered me most because when we drove to Atlantic City every summer we passed a fenced nudist camp, and Dad always cracked an off-color joke about the camp. But I did want to graduate, so off came the trunks.

I quickly mastered diving into the pool from the edge, head first, but I must admit, it was a long way down to the water from that ten-foot high board. I passed the final test by rolling over on my back on the long swim as I gasped for air. I never learned that breathing thing. The dressing room at the gym had a sauna, and that was the thing I remember most about my semester in the pool.

Fast forward to the Sixties. Our weekend summer home had a man-made spring-fed half-acre pond where we all swam in the summer. The children and Marian swam like fish for hours. I would occasionally swim out to the float and rest there. But except in late July when the water warmed, the pond always seemed too cold for enjoyment. So, I paddled around in the rowboat looking for frogs most of the time.

Years later on cruises, I never worried about a big boat sinking, but I would think about falling overboard.

But, I knew I could flip over and float on my back like an otter…at least for a little while.

GUILT

A friend defined guilt in the following way: When the boss calls and says, "Get in here, right away," and doesn't tell you the topic, that feeling is guilt. What have I done?

What do I feel guilty of at this very moment? Answer: I haven't practiced the piano in almost a week. I'm way behind in getting started with the next book club book, "Dutchess of Death." I've wasted most of this day playing games on the computer.

All in all, none of this guilt amounts to much. Not enough to keep me awake tonight. In fact, I once read a serious article entitled, "The Creative Uses of Guilt," suggesting that a touch of guilt can be an incentive to spur action when dawdling is a block.

Sometimes, a healthy measure of guilt is appropriate. Tiger Woods might be feeling a ton of guilt at the moment for a ton of indiscretions. At least he says feels guilty for what he has done. Is his remorse real, or just an immediate response to his recent psychotherapy and his long range business plans? We can be certain that he has hired a host of crisis managers who are losing sleep trying to figure out how to rehabilitate one of the finest and richest golfers of all times.

His is a special case; an only child given intense attention by his parents, particularly his Dad. Tiger says that he believed the rules did not apply to him, because he was so special, so gifted. It is rumored that his Dad was a philanderer. If true, might there have been a subtle message to the young man that indeed, he could make the rules for himself? We may never know.

Trying to be honest about what I have done through the years that is a legitimate cause for guilt…one or two items come to mind. I rarely lose my cool, but I have lost my cool occasionally, and every time I have flown out of control, I feel deeply guilty about it when I do. My first defense is to believe that I had cause to shout or point fingers. But my satisfaction doesn't last long and guilt remains. Once or twice in my life I have put my fury in writing, only to have wise mentors tell me that there was a better way to respond to my frustration.

Talking about guilt might make readers feel uncomfortable. That is why psychotherapists have the training they do, so that they can help their patients deal with guilt without harboring related guilt themselves.

Last week I asked Marian if we had any fig newtons in the house. At our next trip to Safeway she bought me a package of those wonderful cookies I love. When we got home I ate at least ten of them in one sitting, an act of outrageous culinary debauchery. My next glucose test revealed that my glucose level had reached nearly 500 mg, or six times normal. Did I feel guilty? You bet. But I am eating one delicious fig bar as I type this. One can overcome guilt by pushing through it.

Weighty Problems

My brothers, Jack and Jim, inherited Dad's body configuration... heavy set, not too tall, built low to the ground. They played guards in high school and college football. I inherited my mother's rather short and lightweight frame. To add to the "little" perception, I was always the "little brother" because I came along five years after they did.

Being the "little brother" had it's assets and liabilities. My hungry brothers were always trying to grab some food from my plate. "Look at the submarine," one would shout, and looking up, my pork chop would disappear. I was a poor eater anyway, as mother often testified, I was raised on peanut butter and milk. I never seemed to weigh very much. I think I was forty pounds for three years. When I married in my mid-twenties I weighed 129 pounds. Marian has always enjoyed telling friends that she had to buy my underwear in the boys department at Lazarus.

As a matter of fact, I did not start to put on weight until I was married, when I was plied with good food.

Being skinny gives one a body image of a thin man's mind in a thin man's body.

I never thought much about weight and it's consequences, except that I was the football manager, not a football player. In college I was a coxswain, not an oarsman. That's what little twerps did.

Then slowly I started gaining weight. I spent the great majority of my adult life in the 170/180 pound range. My Type II diabetes appeared when I was 40. My first Rx for insulin was 12 units of R a day. When I reached 220 pounds I was taking in excess of 300 units per day and completely dependent on insulin to live a normal life. That meant that I was a fat man with a thin man's mind. It never occurred to me to diet. Exercise seemed to have no impact on weight. In fact, I think it made it worse as hunger was a constant companion. I can remember buying candy bars to inhale after work so that I wouldn't eat too much supper. That didn't help a bit because I ate the pizza anyway.

When I became 78 years old, I was diagnosed as having scoliosis and an arthritic spine. At times the pain would be severe. Janice opined that I was not a good risk for surgery, and we decided to go the pain management route, rather than having back surgery. A non-addicting, long acting opiate was ordered named Ultram, and it works like a charm. One small pill in the morning, and I am almost pain free all day. However, it ruined my appetite. For a while I was losing a pound a day, and I have gone from 220 pounds to 170 over the past year. The need for insulin has been substantially reduced.

I have had to buy new pants, and a new belt too. Slowly I am becoming a thin man in a thin man's mind again. But as a "little brother" I was always protected. Who is going to protect me now? Barack Obama?

I think not. I am on my own.

My Kind of Town,
Geneva Is

During the early 1980s I was assigned twice a year to fly to Geneva in May to attend the annual World Health Organization General Assembly, and also the fall meeting. The sessions were a week long, and all in all I traveled about eight times to the city. After two or three trips I began to feel at home, especially enjoying the old town, its shops, restaurants, art museums and other tourist attractions.

If I was accompanied by a business compatriot, we stayed at the Noga Hilton or the Beau Rivage on the north side of the lake. Both are over-priced predictable places. The Noga is a post war spacious hotel with all of the expected amenities. The Beau Rivage was prewar-luxury, and snooty. I usually took a long walk after dinner, and began to look for a smaller, more personal boutique hotel with some real character.

I found one, the Hotel de Armures, deep in the old town, next to the armory and across the street from the city hall. It was a 17ᵗʰ century building that had been converted after the war. Thick walls, beamed ceilings, a restaurant attached, and a fantastic continental breakfast of fresh squeezed orange juice, rich coffee and four kinds of bread….a croissant, a hard roll, a sweet roll and some solid multigrained sliced bread with mountains of butter. The tray also included several cheeses, some fruit, crackers, and a small silver vase with a rose in it.

The food in Geneva was "to die for," as New Yorkers say. The high end restaurants served memorable continental food, but so did the chains like Movenpick. A hamburger ordered there comes rare with a generous serving of sour cream on top, with delicious carmelized onions topping the sour cream. The fondues at the Armures restaurant caused me serious problems, because I always overate, and I would feel stuffed and slightly nauseous for two days.

Even the cafeterias at the World Health Organization served notable food, including a gracious wine list. If you took a guest to lunch there you would reserve a table at the sit-down restaurant (on the top floor overlooking Lake Geneva) with linens, fine china and waiters in tuxedos. Even the simplest lettuce salads seemed always to have the perfect vinaigrette dressing.

Those trips to Geneva twice a year were not much more than paid vacations in a heavenly place. In time I learned every inch of the city center. However, my French was lousy, a definite liability, as I learned.

The first time I had reservations at the Hotel de Armures (The Hotel of the Armory) I deplaned, found my bags and a taxi and announced plainly that I would like to be transported to the Hotel de Amores. The taxi driver turned around and started laughing. I repeated the instruction, but he seemed confused. I pulled the reservation from my billfold...the Hotel de Armures. I quickly learned to pronounce the name of the hotel properly, with the accent on the first syllable.

Hmmmm. What if he had followed my instructions?

A Gallon of Pain Killers

My army assignment in Germany was to run a small medical clinic for an infantry battalion. When we were on base in the kaserne (the German word for barracks) my platoon managed sick call every morning. Our physicians were German. All the others in the platoon were American soldiers. When we went into the field, we set up a battalion aide station. The Battalion was billeted in an old castle in Butzbach, north of Frankfurt. The clinic was a two story modern building adjacent to the castle. The medics occupied the first floor, and the dental facility was located on the second floor.

When I arrived for my assignment I was given the combination to a large safe in which controlled substances were stored. The largest item in the safe was a huge pickle jar of codeine tablets to be used in case we were attacked by the Russians, and casualties required pain killers. When we went to the field on bivouac, the jar would be taken along and closely guarded.

Official procedures required that twice a year I was to count the pills, and make a written report to regimental headquarters.

You've seen these big glass jars in delicatessens…gallon jars in which dill pickles are sold. The codeine pills were a bit smaller than a normal aspirin , white and dusty. The jar had hundreds and hundreds of pills.

The counting procedure would take me at least a day. I was a conscientious rascal, and I accepted the task with great seriousness. In fact I was fearful that if I didn't do it correctly I might be court marshaled for mishandling the controlled substance. I worried that I would lose count half way through and have to start over again. Then too was the fear of theft or chicanery by someone on my staff, although I never shared the combination to the safe with anyone.

I had a serious problem. The weight of the pills on top of the heap would crush a few pills at the bottom of the pile. Every time I counted, a lower count would result. So, every time I counted the pills I would carefully brush up the dust and shattered pills, and put the powder in an envelope. I would forward my report with the envelope stapled to the report. After sending my biannual findings, I would wait anxiously for some sort of reaction from Regimental Headquarters. None ever came in two years. I have no evidence that anyone ever read my paperwork.

The strange part of the story is that no one ever told me how to prescribe the drug. Did I offer one pill? Two pills? Or, a handful of pills? And what would happen if the patient couldn't swallow? I hope that today's medics are better equipped and trained than I was.

I stocked one other codeine-containing medicine… elixir of terpin hydrate with codeine for coughs. The mixture also contained a little alcohol with a touch of chloroform. The ranks loved the stuff, and would come into sick call coughing and hacking, explaining that they needed a bottle of the tasty stuff right away. We never had any instructions about its use, so we prescribed the elixir liberally.

I am sure it soothed those sore throats successfully. At least that is what the same soldiers told me, over, over and over again.

GLOBAL POSITIONING SYSTEMS, AS EXPLAINED BY MARIAN

We now live in the Saratoga Retirement Community's Assisted Living facility. Living is Assisted Living means that we all have limitations in some way, needing some help to get along each day. Some of the limitations are physical, some are various stages of mental issues, normally forgetfulness.

This is not an example of some of those limitations. It is, rather, a story about my wife Marian, and her role as teacher...science, math, etc. To be respectful, the names have been changed, but you will understand.

The other night, Marian and I were late to dinner. The tables for two where we usually sat were full. Just inside the door two residents sat opposite one another. Two empty chairs seemed the place to sit, and we joined the others.

One resident was Bea. Bea has memory problems, best typified by the fact that after she orders, so can no longer remember what she ordered, and dinner is always a surprise for her. She is talkative and distant, and hearing loss requires that you must repeat things several times. Lynn is different. She never talks. When the waiter comes to take her order, she points to her selections, and the staff is smart enough to go with the flow. Sometimes Lynn will respond to a direct question with a one word answer, or a nod of the head.

Bea: "Did anything interesting happen today?"

Tom: "We went to a family reunion."

Bea: "Where was it?"

Tom: "In San Francisco."

Bea: "I don't know where that is."

Marian, listening carefully, decided to add to my information. I have a GPS unit in the car. I programmed it in our parking lot. Soon after we left our campus, the lady's virtual voice announced that we had lost satellite contact. I was not worried because we had a long way to drive before we needed it to navigate the streets of San Francisco to find the Hotel Huntington on Nob Hill. Just before we arrived at the city's edge, the voice said, "Get off at the Seventh Street ramp, and turn left." I missed the ramp, and we wandered around a while until the GPS came back on. Eventually, we got to the hotel just at the appointed time.

Marian: "We had trouble with our GPS device."

Bea: "What's that?"

Marian: "A Global Positioning System."

Bea: "Spell it." (Marian spells it.)

Bea: "I don't know what that is."

Tom: "It's a device that tells you where you are."

Bea: " How does it work?"

Marian: "It works on a satellite."

Silence. Lynn has not said a word, or even showed any interest. After a while, Bea who had been thoughtful and silent said, "What's a satellite?"

Fortunately, dinner arrived at that moment, and the conversation was over. But I really would have liked to hear Marian tell Bea what a satellite is.

To Was or Not To Was,
That Is The Question

"To be, or not to be" is NOT the question. Things have changed, and we ponder the past...what we once were, and are no longer. We are still the person we were, but not quite.

For example. I was once a son. Now both my parents are dead, and I no longer worry about whether Mother was eating enough. Or, that Dad would be home in time to "go for a ride" after dinner. As Mother's Alzheimers progressed I became as parent to my parent and arranged for her transfer to assisted living.

I was once a businessman, but I retired in 1993, years ago. I no longer know anyone who works for the company. Most businessmen worried about the sales gains, the budget, the personnel, and the long range plans. I never worried about any of that. In fact, they sent me to a course at Harvard to learn how to read fiscal reports. The only thing I remember about the course was that one night after dinner, we were watching television and Barry

Goldwater made his famous retort, "Extremism in defense of liberty is no vice." At the time I wondered whether I really heard him properly.

In preparation for the trip to the Harvard Business School I bought a new sport coat, a night watch tartan plaid. That coat has long since disappeared, like so many of the other artifacts of a previous business life…brief cases, passports, luggage, knick knacks from my desk…all gone.

I was once a father, and still am, but things have changed. The "children" are now fifty years old and our relationships have changed. They have become as parents to their parents. The telephone calls are more about how we are getting along and how our health has improved or worsened. And whether Marian is eating enough.

One of the only serious arguments I have ever had with my younger daughter concerned the keys to my car, and the suggestion that I was not competent to drive. We started to argue, and then shout, and I grabbed my car keys back. How dare she? It was so bad that her husband called the next day to tell me that "She really loves you, and was expressing her concern. She is not well (the guilt trip thing thrown into the discussion.) and that I was too thoughtless." "But she was out of control." I argued.

That argument is all behind us with almost no scars, but it does reveal that things are not as they once were; my "was" has changed. Janice still frets when I drive at night, or in the rain. And of course, at some point I will have to give her my car keys, BUT NOT NOW.

We are bound to our past seamlessly, but some days it doesn't feel that way. The responsibility is gone, the daily obligations are gone, even the coat and tie are gone. It's wonderful.

TO BE OR NOT TO BE...
A RESPONSE BY JANICE HUDSON

To quote Dad's version: " To be or not to be' is NOT the question. Things have changed, and we ponder the past.... What we once were, and are no longer We are still the person we were, but not quite."

I once was a child, considering my parents as the source of love, learning, and safety. They lovingly and patiently taught us how to be adults, well, sometimes: there was that night we sneaked out to the midnight movies. Oh, and the party at our house when the folks were in Tahoe. And, uh, well, many other incidences of bad behavior. I am now a woman, am grateful for what they taught us. And they are now my friends, and still the people I still look up to, and admire. At the same time, they're cool, and fun to hang out with.

I once was a nurse, but changed the type many times. Open heart ICU. Got bored. ER, got burned out. Flight nursing: fun, but not the kind of job to retire from at age 65. Nurse Anesthetist, the best job in the world, (except that four letter word "call"). Now I'm 'retired', or formally labeled as 'disabled'. Funny, I don't feel disabled. Well, sometimes.

I once loved to show horses, dressage, the most formal and exacting sport in the equine world. An unusual choice for my personality type. Generally speaking, I'm not interested in the tiny details, but rather the big picture. No one could ever accuse me of loving formal clothing, In fact I detest it. But it now seems to be way too much trouble to dress up and ridiculously expensive to show horses- all for a $2 slash of ribbon.

I once was a single woman, and loved my independence and freedom. Now I am married to a wonderful man, (most of the time), and cannot imagine drinking in clubs until 3am. Sounds awful. As a married woman, I still have my independence and freedom, but in a better way. The joy and comfort of a happy marriage (when he doesn't need a killin') is the most important thing in my life.

I once was a working woman, and loved all of what I did. When 'retirement' was forced on me, I had to hack away a large part of my identity. In its place, a whole new world is open to me. I never have enough time to follow all my interests, which are now wide and varied.

I once spent my professional life caring for others. Now, my job is to care for myself. In the medical profession, we put our patients before everything. Our basic needs- sleeping, eating, even going to the bathroom. It is difficult to let go of that indoctrination and treat myself the same way I have cared for thousands of patients over 30 years.

My sainted mother always was brimming with little tidbits. One of them was "Life always changes", and "Sometimes, life isn't fair". These little snipits used to be annoying. But, as expected, she was always right. Life guarantees change, but with it we bring all the wisdom we have attained over the years. It is said 'youth is wasted on the young', and I now understand. At 50, I finally have enough life experience and wisdom, but my body can't keep up.

MUSIC, MUSIC, MUSIC

Once a week in elementary school the teacher rolled in a phonograph and played some program music under the rubric, "Music Appreciation." We listened to "Night on Bald Mountain, "The Sorcerer's Apprentice" or "Till Eulenspiegel's Merry Pranks." The teacher related the story, and we were to imagine the events as they occurred, including Till's hanging.

My family thought I might have some musical aptitude. After family Sunday dinners at the paternal grandparents I would sneak out after dessert and pound on the living room piano until Aunt Velma rescued everyone with a song or two. As a consequence, Mother and Dad bought me a spinet piano when I was eleven. Dad talked about sending me to the Curtis Institute for serious lessons, but instead they hired a woman who played piano in a bar.

Her approach was to have her pupils play real tunes, simplified, but recognizable melodies. She never introduced scales, exercises or any of the essential basics. I loved it and practiced three or four hours a day. After a while she introduced me to stride piano and sheet music with the tunes of the day. Mother had a sweet soprano voice and would sing along when I played a song she liked. I sang too. One day she was standing behind me listening, and she blurted, "Your father couldn't sing either."

Nonetheless, I joined the junior high school choir, and was selected to sing in an octet. Our big number was "When Day is Done" that we sang during concerts. My music lessons continued with Mr. Arnold, the junior high choir director. Before too long I could play a passable "Clair de Lune" and "Golliwog's Cakewalk." My secret… practice, practice, practice each phrase, but never sight reading the music as I played. Everything by memory.

The next major step was learning to play a Hammond organ. One summer I worked on a road gang during the day, and took music lessons with radio personality Melody Mac on the Hammond organ at night. Lessons comprised mostly of playing modern and show tunes up to speed as he played piano and I struggled along at the console. In time I could play well enough to obtain a job in a small bar on Wednesday and Friday nights, and at a roller skating rink on Saturday and Sunday. My gimmick at the bar was to have a spinet next to the organ. I could play a melody on the piano with my right hand, and the organ with my left hand and feet. Frankly, by legitimate musical standards I was faking it, but at seven dollars an hour I was making a fortune for a college student.

When I was drafted, the chaplain at Camp Cooke, California had me play the organ for Wednesday night prayer service, and Sunday church services. I insisted on having hours and hours of practice because I still didn't sight read: how convenient in basic training-barracks environment.

After discharge I moved to a bachelor pad in Columbus, Ohio and began a record collection, primarily classical. I met an attractive young lady who sang in the Broad Street Presbyterian choir. Under the guise that I came to drive her home I soon was a member of the baritone section. The choir was a large one, 85 voices. The director, Dick Johnston, was a voice professor at Capital University and was trained in conducting by Pierre Monteux. The choir sang the great liturgical literature: Bach, Handel, Brahms, Mozart, etc. We performed the Verdi Requiem with an orchestra and organ, and of course, "Messiah" every Christmas and the Faure Requiem at Easter. I still didn't sight read very well, and sat next to someone who could, and sang along enthusiastically.

We bought season tickets to the Columbus Symphony and the Columbus Opera. The symphony wasn't very good, but they had first rate soloists: Isaac Stern, Eileen Farrell, Yehudi Menuhin, etc. After our daughters went off to college we built a new house on our weekend farm. We installed a decent audio system, and had music on whenever we were home. I bought all the symphonies of Mahler and Sibelius and played them ad nauseum.

After seven years of applying we obtained tickets for two Wagnerian operas at Bayreuth, Germany... "Tristan and Isolde" and "Tannhauser." That trip was one of the highlights of our musical lives.

When we moved to the Saratoga Retirement Community I wondered if I might have any of my keyboard skills remaining. We bought an electric piano with bells and whistles...rhythm section, 37 voicings AND ear phones so I can practice without disturbing anyone. It has been disappointment. I have had a stroke and the previous paralysis of my left hand restricts movement, I practice a little, but enjoy the memories the practice evokes.

And, I still can't sight read. Damn !

AFTERWORD

These small pieces have been written to be read aloud to the writer's group at the Saratoga Retirement Community. They are influenced by the writings of James Thurber who could be amusing and entertaining in a short form. He is my writing hero, ever present, although I hear someone saying, "You are no James Thurber."

In fact, I have a mini-Thurber museum in my bathroom. Over the commode is a large photograph of Thurber, mostly blind, lighting a cigarette, reminding me daily that he once set an apartment on fire. To my left is an original Thurber cartoon with a small sleepy dog. The cartoon refers to a soap opera that preempted a baseball game, to the disgust of the listeners.

I have never determined whether the cartoon was ever published, but suspect it might have been in a small, left-leaning topical tabloid called "PM" for which Thurber made an occasional submission. I know the newspaper, because my Dad was a political editor and had the paper mailed to our home. I always looked at the comics it contained.

Opposite the washbasin is a reproduction of a New Yorker Thurber cover dated February 9, 1946. The cover is a mélange of Thurber dogs, each breed magically distinguishable from the other.

Next to the shower is the TIME cover dated July 9, 1951, believed to be Thurber's last self portrait. Beside the shower is a framed sheet of $.29 memorial stamps issued on his 100th birthday.

This book is probably my last self portrait, unless I publish "The Best of VIN YETS AND COMMENTARY."

Tom McCollough
Saratoga, California, 2011